DANCING WITH JESUS

A Story of Schizophrenia

Mimi Whittaker

Dedicated to the Memory of

Grace Chowne Gale and
Francis Xavier Savage,
two of my great-grandparents.

To the Reader:

This is a work of fiction based on a true story.
All of the names have been changed.
I have imagined certain events
that convey the emotional truth of the story.

ACKNOWLEDGMENTS

The writing of this book spans over 20 years, some of the people I first acknowledged have since passed on. Thanks to those then and now

To Guy Biederman for editing and tirelessly encouraging the story - thank you.

To my husband, Gordon, thanks for the space and time and for suffering many a crappy dinner while I wrote instead of cooked.

 To Shirlee Johnson, who is still encouraging me all these years.
Thanks, Susan Weinstein, for your loyalty and friendship and poet's eye.

From the early days:

Thanks to my brothers, Brian and Harry Gale for getting me the Dictaphone I needed to get started on this project and to the rest of my family, Rowland and Isabel Gale, my parents, and Cindy Crawford (not the one you're thinking of), my sister. To my son, Evan, thanks for your help and for being the best son in the world. Also thanks to Pat Voss for helping me get started in the original typing of the book (word processor with 5 ¼" floppy!). Thanks also to my many, many friends who have lent words of support in spite of their fears or anxieties, Linda Wix, Rosemary and Don Perdue, Susan Miller, Fran Zepeda, Jack Trowbridge, Phil Hauseman, Wayne Vieler, Ina Lejins, Tom and Robbie Danchuk. Special thanks to my friend, Jerilu Breneman for her practical help with the computer. Also to Barbara Luchte...thanks to her I've maintained a semblance of sanity. Without Ann Hauser, I might never have had the courage to publish, thank you, Ann. To beautiful Ellen, whom I deeply admire. To Susan and Bob Polovetz for their straight talk and protection. And thanks to Chris Carmignani who was a friend in this phase of my life. Also, thanks to Jennifer Kaiser for her many skills and helps.
Thank you, my dear friend, Linda Carroll, you've been my champion all of my life. Words are not enough.

Most of all, thank you to my mentor in life, Daisaku Ikeda, who has been an inspiration in how to live a life with no regrets. I dance joyfully on to fulfill my mission. Thank you, Sensei!

Table of Contents

"Once in a golden hour I cast to earth a seed;
up there came a flower the people said a weed."

Tennyson

Chapter One   Meeting

Petaluma sits like a cowboy in the saddle of Sonoma County. Rolling hills of dairy and chicken farms sidle up to the river where the town first grew up. Built strong, out of wood and bricks, country music is the breath of the town, the mortar in the walls. In '93 Joni put on the boots she had bought two years before.

"Sorry, I can't make it tonight – I have to watch the grandson," was her friend, Barbara's response to yet another invite to go to dance lessons.

"I don't dance," was Shirlee's response.

Susan was too wrapped up with her boyfriend, Jerry. And on and on. This time Joni was going even if she went alone. This time those polished boots were going to get scuffed up.

She was determined to learn some new steps. I'm going to dance tonight come hell or high water, she thought. She wasn't a redneck, in fact, she was a practicing

Buddhist. Country music, though, had grown on her and she would sing along in the car as she drove the half hour south to Petaluma *All my exes live in Texas...* was especially poignant after her two failed marriages.

Steamer Gold's was upstairs in the old mill by the river. She clomped up the wooden stairs her heels clicking sharply on each step. On the landing she looked out the large window at the street below. Across the road was McNear's bar. They had live music, but there wasn't much of a dance floor. Everyone had told Joni that Steamer Gold's was the place to learn to dance. There were lessons seven nights a week followed by both line and couples dancing. Joni jumped in with both boots.

She got a small table by the dance floor off to the right. Nursing a diet coke, she took in the scene. Cowboy hats lined the bar, the single men. They all wore jeans and most had fancy Western shirts on. Some wore tee shirts, but they all seemed to know each other. Leaning with backs to the bar, beers in hand, they surveyed the dim room.

Women sat in around tables, chatting and laughing. Discreetly eyeing the bar for prospects, they all seemed to know each other, too. Most wore skirts that flared out in the turns, the rest had on tight fitting jeans. Everyone wore cowboy boots.

Her first time there, a few weeks before, she was early. Like the times growing up and moving to new schools, the familiar feeling of being a weirdo, a freak had paralyzed her. She sat against the wall at a table on the dance floor leaving as little space as possible to cross when dances ended and she had to sit down.

A guy in jeans and a blonde mullet was alone on the dance floor. He talked to himself stepped and turned in the dead air, grape-vined to nowhere. Joni thought he looked a fool. Then he announced it was time to start the lesson. She was the fool. After that, she had come to like Wayne. Everyone liked Wayne. His girlfriend, Ina was a beautiful lithe blonde encouraged new dancers.

"Would you like to dance?" Joni startled and looked up. She recognized him - the man wore tennis shoes in a sea of cowboy boots. She had danced with him before, but only remembered his shoes. He was tall and thin with sunken eyes. Shy, but neatly dressed in khakis and a plaid button down shirt. No cowboy shirt like the popular black with orange flames or the Roy Rogers Vintage. His face defied a definite age. Younger than she, for sure.

"What are we doing?" Joni asked.

"I don't know - a slow dance, I guess." he said. Voice was gentle, the kind of sweet that is disarming without being sugary. His hands trembled slightly at her delicate touch. At just over six feet tall, he towered over her five foot frame. She had to watch her steps to keep up with his stride. "Slow, slow, quick, quick," Joni mouthed to herself trying to keep the rhythm and not get tangled up in his feet.

She stumbled on many of the turns, but he was very patient though somewhat expressionless. An understatement. He *was* expressionless...not somewhat, but a whole lot. It was hard to tell if he had been ordered to dance as a bizarre

3

penance or if he had actually come voluntarily. She found him interesting; he was so quiet and yet so patient and gentle.

As she danced around, she saw another man attractive and very outgoing. They made eye contact. He soon came and asked her to dance. His name was Keith. Joni thought he was almost too attractive with his muscular build and beautiful green eyes. The night went on with these two men taking turns dancing with her. She fell victim to the arrogance of beginners' luck thinking that it would go on this way indefinitely - it didn't. But, this night she had a wonderful time in spite of the fact that her heart was still in pain. Dancing was healing for her. Over the days that followed, she thought about the two men, Karl and Keith. Karl was the more quiet man (the tennis shoes man) and she thought to herself, he's not that attractive; he is either an idiot savant or a rocket scientist. I can't figure it out. Keith, on the other hand was very attractive physically. He seemed like a very nice man, but there was something about the way he moved in on her that made her uncomfortable. She did not want to be somebody's girlfriend - not yet, not so fast.

Maybe it was the distance in him that made Joni more interested in the quiet man. She returned week after week, he showed interest in her as well. She stumbled often in her movement around the floor, but he never complained and would patiently help her when she asked for help. He never tried to correct her without her solicitation.

One night Wayne announced after the lesson that Karl danced every dance. Not only did he dance every couples dance, but every line dance. He knew them all. We all applauded this accomplishment because there were so many steps to remember. Each line dance had its own set of steps and very few dancers could do them all.

During one dance, Joni said to him, "you must be bionic", and he laughed.

4

He said, "Yeah, well I wish I had six million dollars" and she laughed as well. That was the extent of their conversation, but she was becoming aware that he must indeed be quite intelligent - more the rocket scientist than the idiot savant after all. There was a depth that was hard to describe about him; a mysteriousness.

"What's the story on Karl?" Joni asked Wayne during a break in the DJ booth.

"I don't know for sure," Wayne said. "Some people say he was in a car accident and had brain damage, but he's going to school. His books are stashed behind the bar. I think he's okay."

Old Bob also danced with Joni most nights. Some of the more accomplished dancers were too impatient with newbies, but Bob danced seven nights a week even though he had to drive from the town of Sonoma to do it. He was a World War II fighter pilot and short from the broken bones. "I took down seven planes," he told Joni – "and three of them were Germans!" Bob was the floater who danced with every woman in the place. Most were young enough to be his daughter or even granddaughter. He had a new old joke almost every night, too. His specialty was teaching the 'Y' dance.

Grabbing the unsuspecting Joni around the waist he said do you know the 'Y' dance?

She laughed – "no", so he said, "I'll teach you – come closer" and she moved in to him a bit. "Closer! "He said a little louder. Laughing she got in closer. "Closer! "he said louder. By now she was laughing as he hugged her to his chest and he said softly, "Why dance?"

Many nights Karl would walk her to her car and kiss her respectfully good night. "Where are you parked?" she had asked the first time they walked out together.

"Oh, I walk." He had replied quietly and then dropped the subject. "You must live nearby," she had ventured another time.

"Yes," he had half-chuckled, "not far at all." Again he didn't elaborate.

If he wanted me to know where he lived he'd tell me, Joni thought. Still, she was curious.

Finally, after several months she decided to really thank him for his patience and help in teaching her new steps. She asked him to go out for coffee. He accepted. When they sat down across from each other she excitedly said, "Tell me about yourself. Who are you?" Her fascination bubbled out.

He looked at her with his eyes slightly rimmed in red and hesitantly said, "I am the reincarnation of Jesus Christ".

Her heart sank. Now is a good time to get up and run, she thought, but she didn't. Something made her stay, glued to the seat of the booth. The table was too high for her, so she was leaning forward, arms across her chest and resting atop the table. She was blown back against the seat with this comment, but tried not to overreact. She looked him straight in the eyes trying to discern whether he was joking. He wasn't.

You sure know how to pick 'em she said to herself as she listened further for signs that he was kidding.

"I am going to be unifying all the world's religions", he said matter-of-factly. It is very big. I am going to be very big. Do you know Ramakrishna?"

6

"No," she said. *Keep an open mind she thought. Listen carefully.* "Well, he was a guy who lived in India. I was him too, you know."

Looking at him squarely, Joni said, "I really do think that you do have an important mission in life."

Karl hesitated a bit and then went on. "You know, really, my family name is going to be very big. My parents don't know it. They don't understand, but that's what is happening; I can hardly believe it myself."

"Where do your parents live?"

"Have you ever heard of a place called Minneapolis, Minnesota?" He asked furtively, as if she would not have heard of such a place unless she had some secret knowledge.

"Yes," she said without extra comment. *Is he for real?* She thought to herself. *Does he think I'm stupid? Have you ever heard of a place called Minneapolis? Does he think I'm from another planet? Is he being polite or condescending?*

"That is where they are," he said.

"Oh", she said that's nice and how long have you been here?" The conversation went on regarding vital statistics - how long they had been where. It turned out he had a four year college degree and had studied for eight years under Eknath Easwaran in Tomales, California, not far from where they sat at that moment. He had tried to be a devotee of the guru, but was thrown off the ashram for "working too hard". She would figure out all of the details of this later. For now, she just wanted to understand what was going on with this man who was kind to her, intelligent, and yet lost in space.

7

Her heart was pulling her to leave, get away as soon as possible, but she was somehow intrigued on the other hand to learn more about him. They talked a bit longer and then got up to leave. She asked if he wanted to go for a walk and he said that would be a good idea. So they walked, and as they walked into the neighborhood at night, she thought to herself, *What am I doing? Why am I walking on a dark street alone with this man who is obviously crazy?*

"Would you like me to carry your purse for you?" he asked innocently, boyishly.

"No thanks, I'm fine." That would be the last thing she would want to do, and yet he seemed genuine and harmless. They walked a bit and suddenly she felt uneasy.

"I need to go back now."

"Okay," he said, so they turned around. "You know we could try sleeping together." "Oh, no I am not prepared for that."
"It would really be good. It would be really good for you. You know if we slept together you would never have trouble with sex again."

Joni roared with laughter. "What a great line! That is really fantastic. You should write these down for other men. I'm not kidding!"

"You know, I can't have sex." He was placating.

"You can't?" she grinned in reply.

"God doesn't want me to."

"Why?" she asked still smiling.

"Because if I had sex the whole world would have to and there are enough people."

Joni didn't push it; the whole world is having sex, she thought, except for me maybe.

She found him refreshingly humorous and at the same was baffled that he seemed to be serious. They got back to the car and she decided she would drop him off. "Where do you live?"

"Well, right now I am on the street," he said. Again, her heart sank.

"You mean you are living on the street."

"Yes," he said.

His head faced straight ahead, but his eyes darted sideways as she drove. She sensed that he was raw emotionally – couldn't face what was once real. A normal life had vanished and he had no clue as to where or why. *He danced to keep warm*.

Now, what was she going to do? It was cold. Here was this man who wanted to come home with her and she realized it wasn't just an attraction, but a place to stay. She would talk to him some more, feel things out and perhaps get her courage up to just dump him off on the street again. She drove around the block and parked to talk awhile. Somehow hours and hours went by. He kissed her and held her tight and all the while she thought, *this is not going to work, this is not right, I shouldn't do this*, but something about him was so familiar and so mysterious.

Finally, she looked at her watch. It was almost 4:00 am. Canceled the thought of getting him a hotel room. No money for that. She decided to take him home. Just for the night, but inside there was still a reserve of fear. "Okay, let's go home."

"Okay, he said. Do you want to drive or do you want me to drive?"

She looked at him. "Do you have a license?" No response. His face darted away.

She started the car. Immediately she sensed that she had hurt his feelings with her direct and firm question, but she was clear that no one without a license was going to drive her car. Some sense of reason had to prevail. Score one for logic.

The sky seemed closer than usual that night. Three times she saw stars shoot across the sky. "Did you see that?" she said. I've seen three shooting stars tonight. That has never happened to me before." She wondered if this was an omen of something wonderful or something disastrous. Would this be the night she would die or would this be the start of something she had long desired? Whatever it was, it seemed big.

They got home and he reiterated, "Now we have to keep underwear on. That's the rule."

"Okay", she said, not understanding what he was talking about. She slipped on her night gown and left her underwear on; he got into her bed keeping his underwear on.

She snuggled in beside him; sure enough, he anxiously took off her night gown, but never touched her underwear. Somehow, she felt safe even knowing that logically she shouldn't. Their energies seemed to link; to understand on a level just beneath consciousness. Too tired to figure it out, it felt right that he was off the street for a night.

Passionate in his hugs and kisses and held onto her like no one ever had before; almost as if his life depended on it. Still, she was not giving in 100 percent and finally they fell asleep.

The next day came early, several hours later in fact. They spent the day watching a movie and napping intermittently.

"How do you iron your shirts?" She asked knowing it had to be a dumb question, but he always looked so neat and clean.

"I don't." he answered in his usual economical way.

"Well, they always look freshly ironed." She felt from the gentleness in his voice that it was safe to push this far at least. She would drop it if he didn't want to say anything further.

Surprisingly, he comfortably offered, "I go to Goodwill and make an exchange. I take off one shirt and put on another. I don't feel bad, though. I've given a lot to Goodwill over the years."

Joni was amazed. How sane! How simple! "Well, that's what Goodwill is for," she reassured. "I'm sure they wouldn't expect you to pay if you absolutely couldn't."
Enough said. He was going quiet again, so she took the hint. They agreed that the plan was to go dancing again that night and she'd leave him at the club where they met. She did. Once there, he pretended that he didn't know her and danced with other women avoiding her at all costs. She went up to him at one point and said, "You'd better dance with me tonight". *Why did I do that?* she thought.

"Oh I thought you had left," was his weak reply.

"Yeah," she said. "Okay." So they danced a couple of dances, and then she left saying good-bye as he danced by in another woman's arms. *Well, I got out of that one*, she thought as she drove home.

Later that week, she went dancing again. He walked her to her car and smiling said, "We could try sleeping together again tonight".

"No way, Jose! I have to work tomorrow." "Well, you could call in sick, he teased".

"No, I can't. I'm the only one there," she replied. "But maybe tomorrow or the night after...will you be around?"

He shook his head yes.

"Okay", he said, and turned on his heels like a military guard leaving his post and walked away dejected. She felt the pain of his rejection, wanting to take it back, but couldn't. She did not run after him. She wanted to say, it's not so bad, I'll see you again, but she couldn't. She had promised him another night and she meant to keep her promise if only to provide shelter when she could. The thought of how he lived on the street worried her and she was fascinated and curious at the same time.

Two days later she went dancing again. A weekend night. He came in late, and as was their usual routine, they both danced with other people, but tended to dance together a little bit more frequently.

At one point, however, a new couple was there trying to learn the Texas Ten Step.

Joni was showing the husband, Ron, how to do it; taking him around the floor even though he was half drunk. Good naturedly he was trying to learn the complicated steps. All of a sudden, she realized Karl was gone. She ran out soon after and ran across the street to where she thought he was and found him. "Why did you leave?"

He looked at her blankly and started walking with her back toward her car. Again she asked, "Why did you leave?" He said, "Well I sat through several dances, and there wasn't anyone left to dance with, so I left."

"You can come and get me anytime," she said, really sincerely. "At least we should be able to tell each other when we are leaving if nothing else. Okay?" She unlocked her car door. He hesitated. "Are you going to come or going to stay?" she asked, thinking it was understood that he would be coming home with her that night.

"I think I'll stay", he said, rather sadly.

"Okay", she said feeling rejected and hurt, but trying to respect his feelings. She got into her car and drove away as he walked back across the street. *Why do I care?*

This guy is nuts and a loser. Why in the world do I care? She drove home. *This is good. This is good. I do not want this,* she thought. In the weeks that followed, they danced together on and off, still more with each other than with other people. She had picked up some new friends along the way, one of whom was Chris who sat with her frequently, but this did not seem to bother Karl. He still asked her to dance and she still waited for him to ask most of the time. Their friendship seemed stable, but he never again wanted to come home with her and she felt this was probably for the best,

13

although she missed his intense hugs and his gentle sincerity.

Several times he walked her to her car, holding her hand, and kissed her good night, but not always.

November 5 was his birthday. She wanted him to have a nice birthday, but didn't know who else in the place knew that he was homeless. She bought him a pie (because he said he liked pie better than cake) and a card. She didn't know what to give him, because whatever he got, he'd have to carry it with him, so she slipped a ten dollar bill inside the card. He did not show up, so she left the pie and card with Bucko, the manager. The next night she was away at a conference, but apparently Karl did not show up that night either. Then Sunday, the night that he was always sure to show up, everyone was back together and it was a big night for dancing. Someone brought a cake for him and he had his traditional birthday celebration. At Steamer Gold's it consisted of being hoisted in a chair while drinking a shot of tequila. After this everyone of the opposite sex lined up to have a dance with the birthday boy (or girl). The music kept playing until all the women had a chance to go once across the floor with Karl.

"Happy Birthday, Karl, "Joni beamed. She told him about the pie and the card that had been left with the manager, but the pie had gone and no one knew where the card was either.

"Thank you." He was happy to see her and enjoyed the party immensely. She felt really warm that everyone supported him so, even though he was somewhat of an outcast. That night she told him that he was welcome to come and stay for Thanksgiving because she had several days off from work. He said, "Is that next week?"

Joni said, "No, the week after".

"Okay, I'll think about it." They danced on.

The next week she saw him again, but didn't press the issue about Thanksgiving. She'd wait for him to bring it up. It was a normal evening. Inside she ached to learn about life through his eyes. She wanted to spend some time on the street with him. Live as he lived; see what he saw; eat what he ate. She felt a need to understand.
There was a dark freedom that called to her, could she survive? But then, there was the light...of family and friends and people she belonged to. The forces within her were doing battle.

"Children are the anchors that hold a mother to life."

■ Sophocles

Chapter Two   Missing

Finally, it was the Sunday before Thanksgiving. Karl did not show up. Joni planned to go dancing on Wednesday night before Thanksgiving; that's the night he would probably want to come home. Wednesday night came and no Karl. Something was wrong. He never missed a Sunday and now he'd missed a Sunday and Wednesday, two of the most popular nights.

Something is wrong. Well, it must not have been meant to be. Maybe he found someone else to go home with for Thanksgiving or maybe his parents have come and taken him back to Minneapolis. That would be the best scenario possible, but she felt uneasy.

She spent Thanksgiving with her family, but still had a gnawing feeling inside. The day after Thanksgiving she could not wait for the library to open. She decided she was going to track down his parents somehow. She got the Minneapolis phone book out of the library and photocopied the pages with all the Jackson names on it. She did not know his parents first name. It was not going to be an easy task. She decided since

17

there were a finite number of Jackson's in Minneapolis, albeit a large finite number, that she would be able to find out who they were over time if she made ten calls a day or so. She started calling.

She tried to eliminate anyone who sounded like they might be black or have some foreign kind of name, because this guy was definitely a Midwest WASP type. She felt that his parents must be professionals, so she tried the professionals first. She had no luck, but talked to many nice people in Minneapolis who wished her well in her search. Time was ticking away and still he did not show up to dance. Something was very wrong, still she did not know who knew any more about him than she did. Bucko hadn't seen him – no one had – no one was concerned.

She finally went the following week to file a missing person's report with the Petaluma Police Department. They were in the middle of a huge investigation looking for a lost girl named Polly Klaas who became internationally famous. The media was there every night covering this.

"Will you give us a description of this guy?" "Yes, six feet tall, about 160 pounds, hazel eyes." *"Do you have his date of birth?"*

"Well, actually I do.   He just had a birthday.   It is November 5, 1962."

"You don't happen to have his social security number or anything like that, do you?"

"No."

"Where was he living?"

"On the streets."

"Here in Petaluma?"
"Yes."

"How do you know he is missing?"

"Well, he hasn't shown up for dancing and he goes almost every night. He has gone almost every night for a year."

"Where is that?"

"Right down here at Steamers."

"Are you his girlfriend or something?"

"No, I'm just a friend."

"Okay, well we'll take all of this information down. If we find him, though, all we are going to do is ask him if he is okay and make sure that he says he is all right. I know you are trying to help him out, but that's all we can do."

"Will you tell me when you find him?"

"Well, that is not what usually happens, but I could put a note in the file to call you. When we find him, I can tell him to call you."

"He won't do that. He doesn't do phone calls."

"Okay, I'll put a note down and you can call me in a few days or so. I'm sure he's going to turn up in a day or two. You can give me a call. Here's the case number."

She was thankful to get the case number and to have done her part, but she felt that very little was going to be done. This police department was already swamped and as nice as the officer had been, he was talking practically and she did not feel comforted by his words that Karl would probably show up in a day or two. For some reason that did not feel right to her.

In the days that followed, she was contacted by his parents who subsequently sent her pictures. She decided that because she knew he would frequent second hand clothing stores or thrift stores, she would get lists of these stores in the Bay Area. Once she was able to get this list from Goodwill, she sent everyone a flier requesting that if they saw this man to call her or the Petaluma Police. Every day she went to her altar at home and chanted for Karl. Sometimes she would cry more than she chanted, begging the universe to protect his life and send her word that he was safe.

"Joni?"

"Yes, this is she."

"I don't have any word on Karl, except that his parents called to file a missing persons report. I told them you had already filed. I can give them your number if you like."

Joni gave her enthusiastic permission.

Pieces started falling together. She spoke to Karl's father and told him her impressions of what had happened. She was also able to talk to Bucko and the dance instructor, Wayne, at the club who both knew that Karl was homeless and that he had some mental problems going on. Karl's parents had called the club on a regular basis to check on how he was even though he refused to talk to them. The club owners would even allow Karl to steal certain small amounts of money and his father would pay it back. Even though they would discourage it, this was the pattern Karl took.

Bucko was a mountain of a man, a short mountain at that. He had an Irish rosy face with a boyish smile. In truth, it would take three long-armed women to completely encircle him with a hug, but his heart was even more vast. He always seemed very happy to be wheeling around this large frame whose girth seemed to be that of a canvas cage ball like those in elementary school days. Bucko told her Karl had circulated a letter the week before and asked if she knew about it.

"No", she said, "I don't".

"Well, he said, I'll have to get you a copy of it. Karl had been talking crazy about going into some state of enlightenment or something. He wanted somebody to take him into their home to take care of him while he went into this state or something and that it was real crazy; like he as going to glow and all this stuff."

"Oh boy, this is really severe."

"You know, I told him", Bucko went on, "I don't care about anybody's religious beliefs, that's fine, but when it starts interfering with my customers, then I have to draw the line. I told him that was what was going to happen if he continued to bring those things around to show the customers." He said, "You know he is a nice guy and all, and we have been kind of looking out for him for the past year, but I can't have him interrupt my business".

"Oh, I understand", she said, "and I understand he has been stealing".

"Well, he never steals much", Bucko would say. "I guess just what he needs to live. I guess that's part of his religious belief. Like, one time there was thirteen dollars on a table, and he only took like $2.85. He has always taken just what he needs."

"I understand that he is really intelligent from his father."

"Yes", Bucko said, "that is what everybody says. In fact, I think we still have some of his school books in the back."

"Have you got any pictures of him, Bucko?"

"I might, let me look." As Bucko rummaged through, the only picture he could find was one half size picture of Karl dancing with a girl whose back was to the camera. His eyes were closed, but it was clearly him.

"Can I have that?" she ventured.

"Yeah, sure, go ahead and take it."

"Okay, because I am going to make up some posters. I have to find him. I am really worried about him."

"Well, anything I can do to help, let me know," said Bucko.

Joni feared for Karl's life. She had several experiences in recent months where young men she knew had died. Earlier in the year two of her close friends from her Buddhist practice had died; a wife by what some thought was suicide or perhaps an accidental death and then within the two months, the husband. This was a year among other years for her to deeply feel the importance of life and the impermanence of life, the fragility of it. Something in her was spurred to find this man. She felt from the bottom of her life that he was in danger of losing his.

Several days later she talked to the officer again. He had gone out looking for Karl and listed the places he had been. She had already been to most of those places. She had also been down to the soup kitchen and the shelters. People she encountered at these places filled her heart with sadness. She realized that as alone and strange as Karl was, he was not as far out of reach as most of these people seemed to be. Yet, perhaps he was farther because of that. What irony! His intelligence and education could not override his karma to suffer from this illusion, this disease, this confusion. She made an appointment to get guidance from her senior leader in Buddhism, Mr. Nagashima in San Francisco.

The appointment was set for December 9th, a Thursday and it happened to be her 10th anniversary of practicing. She had two Thursdays a month off, so could go down and meet with him during the day. In the back of her mind, she thought that maybe by then she would have found Karl anyway, but she'd still go for the guidance.

She spoke with Claude, the outreach person who had been primed to help because of a letter he received from Karl's parents. He said he'd try to find Karl and bring him in for psychological testing if Karl would agree.

He spent three or four days, or maybe a week searching for Karl in the mornings. "Karl is psychotic and schizophrenic, "he told Joni. Then went on to explain that this is a disease that comes on in early adulthood. Karl needed to be on medication. Claude was optimistic at first, but within several days called again to tell Joni that he would not be able to continue the search; that he was in effect giving up until Karl decided to seek him out.

24

Joni felt alone again. Didn't anyone care? This was a human life in the balance.

She was determined in a way that she didn't fully understand herself. Was she trying to help his parents because they couldn't get him off the streets? Was she trying to bridge some gap between her own pain of having her son living so far away and worrying about him – wondering who was protecting him? Was it some karmic debt she needed to repay? She had no real answers.

Talking long distance was expensive – writing was easier for her anyway. So she agreed to send a letter to Dr. & Mrs. Jackson.

As she wrote to his parents, she told them of Claude's decision to quit looking for Karl that she was chanting for Karl to be found alive and well and get back to them.

December 3, 1993

Dear Dr. and Mrs. Jackson:

I wanted to drop you a brief run down on the last few days' events and to more formally introduce myself. First off, I have spoken with Claude again today and he tells me he will no longer be searching for Karl each day...no problem, I'll do it. I hope to get the police dept. photo today...the one Claude has is very nice, but no one will recognize Karl. I was able to obtain a photo of Karl dancing from Bucko...several people have been able to ID him from it, but, unfortunately, he hasn't been spotted. I have left my phone #'s with Rick at the Armory shelter...he's seen Karl at the soup kitchen and walking along Lakeville highway in the past. Also at McDonald's - although I need to visit at another time of day...night crew did not recognize Karl. Have spoken with several street people - one of whom ID'd Karl...but the trails all run cold. I'm convinced he's left town and will begin searching southward. I will be going to San Francisco next Thursday and will play my hunches there if he hasn't turned up by then.

In my religion, we chant to align ourselves with the positive rhythm of the universe...I know religion is not what you most likely want to hear about, but just wanted you to know that I am chanting 3 hours a day for Karl's safe return to you. I have enclosed the recent speech from our President Ikeda that he delivered at Harvard University. This will give you an idea of my philosophy and demonstrate to you the realistic validity of it all...we don't meditate to transcend our bodies...we live in the here and now. I'm hoping that Karl will eventually follow a more sane regimen...and also feel he is deeply spiritual, so that some practice will probably always be a part of him.

The picture is the most recent one I have of myself and my 15 year old son, Kevin. He is my absolute pride and joy, so I know how wrenching this must all be for you as parents. Kevin lives with his dad in Albany, NY, but spends summers and holidays with me. Karl has not met him yet, but has seen the multiple pictures of him in my apartment. I live in an apartment at my parents' house that had been built for my late grandmother. I had always lived on my own from the age of 18, so it was a shock to move close like that to my parents at the age of 38, but it's worked out just fine.

They're very respectful of my privacy. I am now 40...to turn 41 in February. I was first married at age 20, had my son at 25 and divorced at 27. Remarried at 34 and divorced at 38. So you can see, not a great track record. I told Karl from the beginning that all I wanted out of our "relationship" was to be able to dance together for as many years as we had to dance. I do care for him, but have absolutely no expectations beyond that. You may feel that it was odd that I let him come home with me and sleep in my bed, but in the past 4 years I have only allowed one other man to get that close...and that was over a year ago. Of course, should I become involved with someone my life will change, but for now I am determined to make good use of this time in repaying my debt of gratitude to Karl.

I had tried to "get in to" dancing several times in the past 4 years, but due to various circumstances, not the least of which was a "cold shoulder" from some of the more experienced dancers...I was unable to really commit to it until I met Karl. He was the first one to ask me to dance and even though another man, Keith came and sat with me, Karl still kept asking me to dance...I admired that and I never refused him a dance and I never will. I feel that dancing is a very healthy expression for Karl and really hope that no matter what else happens, he is able to continue that expression in some form.

As I told you on the phone, Dr. Jackson...I had written a poem for Karl before we had talked in depth and he revealed his psychosis to me. Somehow I feel that this earlier impression I had of him is more the true Karl than the one who talks crazy. I'm reading up on schizophrenia...my suspicions were correct...Karl does feel too much. It's not at all that he's unresponsive (which is the appearance of it all), but that he's overwhelmed. Anyway, I'm sure you know all about this.

Here's the poem...normally I keep my poetry quite private, but I wanted you both to be aware of my experience of Karl and know that people do care for him and see him for the good man that he is. By the way...he does have a sense of humor and laughed out loud at the title!

Will talk to you soon!

Sincerely,
Joni

My Left Feet *(10/13/93)*

That first night you welcomed me
and danced with my left feet undaunted –
expressionless and reserved,
I felt your passion for the answers
that can only be found in motion.

Your goodness held me gently and breathed
new life into
my faith in kindness.

Behind the softness in your eyes
I saw the pain that you have long endured...
but you're not broken.

Your courage steps lightly

and your patience counts on softly
and sometimes when I trip you up
as I forget my feet...
I see you smiling.

Thank you for your generosity of spirit.

I wish for you always
true happiness, warm winters,
good music and a long, sweet dance into memory.

       As she wrote, she cried. How can I explain to them why
I feel so compelled? How will they trust me to help? In some
way I know that I am still working through my lost custody of

Kevin. It had been almost 7 years now, but the memory, the picture in her mind always triggered the same anguished tears. A grade B movie she would say in explanation, it was like a grade B movie...there he was 8 years old and slightly small for his age at that. She had gotten the call from her father at work...it was New Year's Eve and the lab where she worked was closing early, they were toasting the New Year with champagne when the call came.

"The police are here", said her father trying to keep his emotions under control.

"How can that be? I just talked to my attorney in New York and he said that they wouldn't get involved since there's a stay on file."

"Well, they're here and Rick is with them, too."

"Have they taken Kevin?" she asked soberly now. They can't do this...her mind raced.

"No, but it's inevitable now."

"I'm on my way."

"Now Joni, I want you to drive slowly and carefully. Drive carefully." he repeated as a command. She knew that he was trying to diffuse the chaos in her mind.

She had started practicing Buddhism 2 years before...and now as she got into her car she couldn't wait to get on the open road and scream "Nam Myoho Renge Kyo!" at the top of her lungs. Her scream reverberated off the windshield and felt as though it had blasted to the ends of the universe awakening all of the gods. Her life exploded as she screamed but her body drove her safely to her parents' home.

"You have to go to the police station to say good-bye to Kevin," they would tell her. "You have to go home, pack your son's bags and bring them to the police station and say good-bye." It wasn't possible. It didn't make sense. Even as she remembered the nightmare of that day, it still seemed wrong. She remembered that Rick had brought a suitcase for Kevin's clothes and how she had wanted to fill it with rocks. But it was locked and he hadn't left the key. Typical. She remembered walking into her house, seeing the Christmas tree still up, with Kevin's toys still underneath and walking up the stairs to his room. She remembered crying as she packed his things making a mental note that he had dressed in his new 49ers uniform that day and that he'd surely want his helmet. She remembered packing for winter weather and putting Gonga, the thumb-sucking toy gorilla on top; the sign around his neck, "Beware Gonga Loves You". It would be the first thing Kevin would see when he opened his suitcase half a world away from his mother.

She remembered going to her altar and taking his handwritten prayer, "I want to live with my mother" as a final hope. She remembered going to the police station, her mother beside her trying to hold her to sanity. She remembered her small blonde child walking toward her down a cold grey hallway through a thick doorway and this was always where she'd stop and cry. She'd hold out his helmet saying she thought he'd want it. He would grab it thankfully and put it on as if to protect himself from further pain. She understood, but wished she had waited to kiss him first. No matter. Now was the time to make him feel as safe as possible above all else. "You and I are going to be together" she would invoke as if from Zeus himself, while her heartstrings entwined with his as they had for many lifetimes. Eternity encircled them, holding power for an instant between two sets of deep blue eyes. And, she remembered walking out the door with no feet left to touch the earth. That night...the most important for Buddhists, New Year's Eve, she had gone to chant in the New Year with friends against her own

30

better judgment. She had disrupted the meeting...lost control and in anger slandered the object of worship, the Gohonzon. Screamed that there was no power in Buddhism. Demanded to know why this had happened to her and cried when no one could tell her. No doubt about it, the worst day of her life...and still fresh in its entirety whenever it surfaced to consciousness.

It was this passion that she brought to her search for Karl. It was this mother's love that so deeply empathized with his parents' pain. Somehow the balance might shift if she could eradicate the negative karma had surfaced in her life. If she could restore a son to his mother, hers could be restored to her. She had to win.

"When we talk to God, we're praying.
When God talks to us, we're schizophrenic."

- Lily Tomlin

Chapter Three   The Mission

"I want to return this photo to Lieutenant Forte and I'd like to leave some of these fliers that I've made up with regard to Karl Jackson," Joni spoke through the bullet-proof glass at the police station. A box of lavender ribbons was left off to the side. She got a fresh one, since hers was tattered and Polly Klaas still hadn't been found. Her flier would look makeshift and amateurish to say the least next to the professional job done for Polly, but it was the best she could do. She hoped that the obvious sloppiness of it would draw attention and work in her favor. She was armed with a stack of them for her search.

"Joni, I got the flier you dropped off," Lieutenant Forte had called her at home, he sounded up-beat. "I arrested Karl."

"What? You arrested him?"

"Yes, a few weeks ago I had to arrest him for shoplifting. When I saw this picture of him in your photo I remembered it."

"Where was he shoplifting and what did he take?" Joni was awash with curiosity.

"Over at Payless. He only took small toilet articles, just the things you'd need to survive on the street. He was a nice guy. He told me how he's got a college degree. He also told me about all of the other stuff he's stolen like food and I guess he took a Walkman from K-Mart. Basically, he's just trying to survive on the street. He's a nice guy."

"What will happen to him now? Do you think this is why he's disappeared?" Of course it is, thought Joni! Why ask?

"It might be," ventured the lieutenant, "he's got a court date for December 9th in Santa Rosa. I think he'll turn up well before then."

"What happens if he doesn't show for court?" Joni needed a thread to hold on to.

"If he doesn't show for court nothing will really happen. There will be a warrant out for his arrest and the next time he gets picked up for shoplifting that will give us a chance to hold him a little longer, but it doesn't mean we'll go looking for him."

"So, you're telling me that even though there could be a warrant out for his arrest after December 9th, it wouldn't create any additional energy toward finding him?"

"That's right."

"What's the point of the arrest and the warrant, then? In other words, even though it's obvious that this guy needs some help, he's got to commit a bigger crime or do something really outrageous to get it?" Joni was not accusatory as much as confused in her questioning.

"I know it sounds bad, but that's just about the way it is. Karl only had about $24.00 worth of stuff. It's got to be over

34

$50.00 to make it a grand theft. And, yes, as far as the mental health people go, they need to see that he's a danger to himself or others in a serious way before they can lock him up. You might be able to get him in for a 72 hour hold."

"He's been in for that, "Joni mused. "He said he'd been arrested and taken to the hospital for observation."

"When was that?"

"I'm not sure exactly. It may have been around the time that his parents were visiting last summer."

"Well, like I said, if he wasn't dangerous they can't hold him against his will. Don't worry, though. We'll find him. You're doing a great job so far!"

"Thanks," said Joni. She was glad to do what she could and she was also certain that if she didn't keep up her search, Karl might not be found. I do hope they're right, though, she thought. Maybe he'll just show up.

"I'll keep you posted," she ended, "I'm going to the city soon and I'll nose around there."

"Okay, good luck!"

"Thanks! Bye."

The system had its hands tied in this case. Maybe the arrest warrant would work...it could be an ace in the hole. Anything could be turned to Karl's advantage, no matter how negative it might seem on the surface.

Finally, it was the morning of December 9th. How do you trap Jesus? Joni planned to tell Karl that his disciples were gathering in Minneapolis. Then to get him on a plane back to

Minneapolis that very night. She hoped she wouldn't be coming home.

"You shouldn't be doing this," her friend, Chris admonished her. He had called just as she was leaving.

"I know, but it's none of your business. I have to," she said. "I know you don't understand, but after the recent burnings of homeless people, I am afraid for Karl."

There had been several incidents where homeless people were doused with gasoline and lit on fire.

"I do understand, Joni, but Karl is not your responsibility. Why are you going all the way to the city?"

"Because Bucko told me that Karl sometimes takes the bus down to San Francisco and he obviously isn't around here. I'm drawn to look for him there – don't try to stand in my way."

She went to San Francisco to meet with Mr. Nagashima. Danny Nagashima was the Territory Leader for the SGI Buddhist organization in Northern California. He was a warm and cheerful Japanese man who was both loved and respected by all of the members due to his sincere heart, wit and wisdom. She told him her story of how she needed to find Karl. Her heart ached inside her throat as she told him how she had to find him because no one else would and she felt his life was in the balance. Mr. Nagashima looked her in the eye. It was obvious that he felt she was out of proportion with her feelings.

"This man will never be someone you will have a relationship with. You know that."

"Yes, she said, "that I understand, but I feel like his life is at stake. It is not that I want a relationship with him. I understand that can't be."

36

He said to her very strictly, "If you do not find this man today, I want to you to give up and stop looking." Her chest tightened. He went on. "You need to find the person that is really going to care for you, really love you and be there for you. I can tell the way you are, you are always ready to give to someone else, but this is the beginning of your next ten years of practice. You need to find the man that should be with you."

"Okay, but this is my last wacky thing!" she said laughing. "I just don't think there is anyone tough enough for me."

"They don't have to be tough, said Mr. Nagashima. "He just has to be sensitive, kind and loving." She did not say anything, but she knew in many ways he was describing Karl, except for the small fact that Karl was nuts.

Finally, he said to her, "I don't want you to go to any dangerous places at night. I want you to be careful. What you need to do now is to chant and do what your wisdom tells you to do."

"Okay", she said.

She had less than 24-hours to produce a result.

She went down to one of the rooms in the culture center that had a Gohonzon where she could chant. As she chanted every nerve in her body was anxious and alive. It seemed like an eternity passed, but only about fifteen minutes had gone by when she decided to go out and start her search. Just outside the doors, she came to the parking lot and approached a trailer that had always been there, but she had never really paid much attention to it before. Some Mexican men stood around talking in Spanish. This was a trailer that had day work for laborers. She went inside and was warmly greeted by the man who was the attendant. She told him she was looking for a man, showed

37

the picture, and asked if he had been there. He hadn't. The attendant did have a list of soup kitchens in the area if that would be helpful to her. Yes, she thought, that would be very helpful. He didn't have an extra copy, but she was welcome to copy them down, so she got out her legal pad and pen and began copying the addresses of the soup kitchens.

There was one listed on Portrero Avenue which was the street she was on. She decided to go to that place first. In the Mission District of San Francisco, everything seemed to be gray or brown, not much color, not many people. Nothing like the downtown area that bustled with business people going to and from important meetings. This was the business side of the ghetto and did not feel welcoming at all. Down the street, everything looked to be closed. She found the door according to her address list, to the soup kitchen, but it seemed to be locked and not a kitchen at all. But then as she walked up the block just a bit, there was an opening like a wooden garden gate almost, and she saw people going in. As she went in, there was a patio area, open, and beyond that a covered area with picnic tables and a huge open air kitchen. She asked one of the men sitting on a bench, who seemed to be one of the workers if he had seen Karl showing him the picture. He said, "No".

She went further into the kitchen and saw a man carrying a huge pot. She asked him if he thought he had seen this person. He looked thoughtfully at the picture and said he thought he had, but to ask Chuck, and motioned to the man toward the back. "Thanks", she said and went over to Chuck.

Chuck took the picture and studied it for a long time. "Yes", he said. "He has been here. He is a quiet guy, isn't he?"

"Yes", this was her first confirmation. She was so excited. "When was he here, do you know? Have you seen him recently?"

38

"Well, I can't really say exactly when, but within the last couple of weeks, I am sure of that".

"Yes, she said, that would be right."

"Well, I know he has been here recently", he said, happily handing back the picture.

"Great, she said, thank you so much" and gave him a flier to post in the back should the man came back.

She talked to several more workers on her way out. One table was a group of men from Central America who had come looking for work, but were unable to attain it. They were so interested in talking to her, asking her who she was looking for. "Is this your brother", said the man.

"No, a friend", she said.

"Oh", said the man with the Spanish accent. "The police want him?", he said.

"No, the police are just looking because he is a missing person. He is not really wanted by the police. I just need to find him."

"Oh", he said and addressing the rest of the table, "this is her brother. She is looking for her brother". They all nodded as if they knew what he was saying. "Well, Petaluma", said the man, noting the word on the flier. "Polly, what happened to Polly?"

It was interesting to her that even here in the soup kitchen seventy-five miles away, the concern among these men was for this young girl that had been kidnapped. Yes, it is true it was a nationally focused crime, but the irony of it all - people associated Petaluma with Polly Klaas, missing person and here she was looking for a man from the same town. As the man said Polly, he made the sign of the cross in some way trying to bless her. Joni thanked him for his attention and went to leave. As she did, a dirty looking all American man said to her, "You looking for somebody?"

"Yes", she said.

"Who'd he kill?" he sneered. She just kept walking.

She went back into the culture center to chant some more. She was only a block and a half away. She was excited knowing that he was out there. "Where are you Karl", she thought to herself. "Where the heck are you?"

She got back inside and began to chant. Tears flowed down her cheeks. She thought about how hard it was for her to be away from her son. She thought about how hard it must be for Karl's parents to be away from him and not know where he was.

She thought about the distance between the sane and the insane, between the world of the housed and the world of the homeless. There was a young blond man sitting close to the Gohonzon. He turned around and saw her tears and asked her what was going on. She briefly explained. It felt strange to her to be talking to this man that she did not know at all. His face looked like he could be her own son projected into the future by about ten years. He said his name was John. "Victory or defeat is in your own perception." he told her. It resonated with her. She had faced the terrible loss of custody of her son seven years before. Her guidance at that time was not to give up. Not to believe she had lost, but after seven years, she was still trying to perceive the value in her losses, now this man was telling her the same thing -

He was trying to alleviate the pain that she would feel if she didn't achieve victory. She knew that it was risky to cling to that hope, but she had no choice. She had to find Karl and she had to do it that day.

After a while, they resumed chanting and soon John left. She continued to chant awhile, but began to feel restless again. She was hungry, time had been passing, but she didn't want to take time to eat. She went into a nearby bread store to get some day old bagels and asked the workers there if they had seen Karl. They had not. They suggested the place next door, which gave work to unemployed people and also the bus depot. She walked all around those blocks, leaving fliers, talking to people; bus drivers, professionals, people in coffee shops. Finally, as she walked along, eating a bagel from the bag, she saw a man with a sign, 'will work for food'. He was a black man, probably in his forties. He had a black plastic garbage bag over his shoulders with a hole cut out for his head. His makeshift rain gear because it was supposed to rain that day. She said, "Do you want a bagel?"

"Yes", he said, "sure", so she gave him one and as he ate she talked to him.

"Have you seen this man?"

"Yeah, I think I have seen this guy", he said staring at the picture in his free hand between bites. "He's been over at the soup kitchen."

"Yes", she said, "thank you very much".

He said, "You ought to go over there and talk to those people".

"I have" she said, "but it is good to get another confirmation". She went on, and spoke to another passerby on

41

the street, but no luck. She wasn't getting anywhere, so she went back to the culture center. Her good friend, Barbara, always gave a fresh perspective, so she called her to see what to do next. On her map of the city the places she could go were endless. The soup kitchens were endless, but he had been there. He had been within two miles of the culture center. Where could he be right now? When would he be coming back?

"Barb, it's Joni. Yes, I've been out down here and they say he was at the soup kitchen but no one's seen him for a week or so."

They talked about different places he could be and about the fact that the day was going by. It was now close to 3:00 o'clock. Darkness would be upon her before 7:00 PM.

"Well, if nothing else," said Barbara, "he did have a court appearance today remember in Santa Rosa."

"Well, I doubt he showed up for that, but I'll try that," she said.

She hung up and called the court. After several transfers, she was able to get through to the right person for the information. "Was Karl Jackson there for his court appearance today?"

"Oh, it is under John Karl Jackson," the clerk said. "Yes, he appeared today."

"He did!"

"Yes. He was given a $75.00 fine."

"Thank you very much", Joni said. She hung up the phone, redialed; "Barbara, you're a genius!" she said. "He was there today! I'm coming back."

42

"Great!" said Barb, "Wonderful! Keep me posted."

Joni hung up the phone and ran upstairs to Mr. Nagashima.

"Mr. Nagashima," she said, "I know where he is. He was in Santa Rosa this morning. I have to go back there now."

His eyes widened in amazement.

"You found him," he exclaimed, "Wow! That is really actual proof." They were beaming.

She was so excited. *"He's alive"* she thought on the drive home. *I'll go straight to Santa Rosa, find him and bring him home for tonight, then get him on a plane tomorrow.* It was Thursday. She had to work the next day, but had planned on calling in if this thing came together for her. She had a wooden chalice wrapped in fabric. She wanted it to look a bit unusual. It was wrapped first in a linen dish towel and then covered over with a gold lame fabric scrap that she had and tied together with a filmy red bow. She wanted it to look like something out of the ordinary and would present it to him as a sign of her understanding of his mission. She thought this would get him on a plane to Minneapolis. She also had a flannel shirt for him. She suspected it had been a long time since he had a new shirt.

Once in Santa Rosa, she went straight for the mall. *Chant and do what your wisdom tells you*, she thought... She was chanting all right. She chanted all the way in the car. *I know he is alive. I have got to find him by 7:00 o'clock tonight. After that, I'll have to call it quits for the night.* She felt exhaustion creeping up on her, but no longer was frustration a part of that exhaustion. *It's just a matter of time now, I'll report to his parents tonight.*

43

She got into town, went to the mall and looked around. No sign of him of course, but somehow she still felt hopeful. She saw two young teenage boys and asked them if they had seen the man in the picture she held. "I don't think so", said the one kid.

The other replied, "He is carrying a green backpack?"

"Yes, she said, that is him", knowing full well in her mind that his backpack was blue, not green. She still felt this was an identification she should follow. "I just saw him outside in the parking lot", the young man said.

"Great" she said, and she ran off in the direction he told her. Once outside, she saw a man walking away at a distance carrying a green backpack, but it was not Karl.

Feeling for her sense of wisdom to tell her which way to go, she walked down the block. Coffee houses were a popular place for him. No luck. She stopped in several businesses and left fliers. No one had seen him within the last few days.

Finally, 7:00 o'clock was upon her. Her feet were tired. She was exhausted - she headed home to the siren call of her comfy bed. She called Karl's parents to let them know that he had appeared in court and that it was just a matter of time before she found him.

"Joni! That's great news – thanks so much!" Donald was on the line and Elaine was listening in on the extension. "We are so relieved to know that Karl is alive. Can you bring him home with you, do you think?"

"That's the plan, but only for a day or two. I hope he can get some kind of help after that."

44

"Maybe if he gets some sleep all will come clearer for him. He's been practicing sleep deprivation and that's not good for brain function, "Donald added. "Do what you can, Joni and call us when he's there."

The next day she went to work as always, but rather than going out to look for Karl again that night she decided to go home and rest still feeling the exhaustion from the search of the day before. The doctor's office was quiet, but she had a lot of billing to catch up on. She liked working alone most of the time, and it helped to be on her own when she was tired and needed to concentrate.

The following morning she was awakened by a call from Karl's father.

"Karl was out at Steamer's last night. I called Bucko." There was desperation in his voice.

"Oh," she said, "I didn't go last night, I was too tired. I'll go tonight and round him up." "Okay, he said. Let me know what happens. Call me when you get him if you can."

"Okay, I will try to do that", she said and they hung up.

Joni was feeling ambivalent. The lines between obligation to her 'mission' to rescue Karl; her need for rest and her own life back; and an underlying resentment that Karl's parents were now depending on her so heavily. *That's another fine mess you've gotten us into, Ollie.*

She had a Buddhist meeting that morning. It was Sophia group, a group of women studying their mentor, President Ikeda's guidance. It involved writing a paper once a month for

45

the course of one year. She had written her paper for this month on Karl and her search for him. She was anxious to get to the meeting even though she was tired. Chris had plans too, so he left early, not fully appreciating the fact that she was going to be looking for Karl that night.

The evening came all too soon and she went dancing as promised. She had the chalice in the back of her car and the shirt behind the seat. She was ready with a multitude of lines she could give to try and gain his confidence so she could get him off the street for the night. In her mind it was a temporary measure. In her mind, his parents would arrange for him to go home right away; or somehow she would be able to talk him into going home. A week, tops, but I it wouldn't take any longer than that....

She went to Steamer's and danced as the night wore on, but Karl did not show up.

She talked to Bucko and several people who said that they had seen Karl the night before. Karl had been there and then had gone across the street to McNear's, another bar where she had never been. Steamer's was the only bar she had been to in over ten years.

At 11:00 she went looking for him. Summoning her best courage and attitude, she walked across the street into the bar. Something guided her to go up the stairs, where the music was coming from. Straight ahead was Karl. He pretended not to see her at first, but she walked right up to him. The first thing he said to her was, "Are you the one who made up those fliers?"

She gulped, "Yes, I am. I was worried about you. I know I shouldn't be, but I was."

"I thought it was you", he said and fell silent. He looked over her head – his eyes not really focused on anything, his head slightly cocked to one side.

She stood there for a moment and then said, "I got your letter."

"I didn't send you any letter" he said shaking his head. He looked at her, annoyed.

She fumbled, "you know, the one you left at Steamer's". She was referring to the note he passed around. It proclaimed he was going into the state of Samadhi. Bucko had told her about it. In it he had said that he needed a place to stay during this portion of his life which would not exceed ten days.

"I want to support you", she blurted, realizing that the word 'support' gave a connotation of financial support at the very moment she said it she wished she could suck back the words. It was not what she meant.

He looked at her and said "Don't talk, don't talk, just listen". He was getting confused by her statements and questioning.

"I have to think about this", he said. "I have to ask God". Then, he went out onto the dance floor by himself. The music in this place was rock and roll. There was a live band. A petite lead singer female in what looked like painted on tiger striped leggings sang and danced. She stepped off the low stage onto the dance floor. He was dancing almost with her, but when she went back up on stage, he danced by himself, stepping and jerking in a weird way.

Between songs, he would come back, stand beside her and when the music started, go back to dance alone. On occasion, two women who were sitting with a boyfriend would get up to dance with him to help him save face. He would smile when they did.

Joni stayed and watched. She was balancing patience to wait for him, with the need to get him out of the place. She wasn't going to leave without him.

Other men asked Joni to dance, so she danced with them one after another. Finally, Karl asked her to dance with him. She obliged. He told her that he wanted to stay until the place closed at 1:30. "That's fine", she said. "I'll wait."

At 1:00 o'clock the band ended and everyone moved downstairs to the bar area.

Only a half hour left. He wanted to stand among the crowd and listen to the conversations, 'picking up messages', as he would call them. She stood silently beside him. Then he said he was going to the men's room. This meant a long walk through a crowd of people to the back of the bar. She offered to hold his backpack. A ransom so that he wouldn't slip away. He came back and stood beside her, not offering to take his backpack, but allowing her to hold it. Unspoken, an attitude that she was enslaved to him. She felt anger underneath the countenance of calm that she wore, but her goal was to get him to safety no matter what humiliation she would have to bear - within reason, of course.

There was something about him, as crazy as he was. She had thought many times about living with him on the street for a time to understand how he lived, how he survived. How he could be homeless and never appear to be? She wanted to know who he was. She wanted to know what made him tick. She wanted more than anything to be able to write about his life or inspire him to write about it, because she felt it was somehow very important. So she stood there silently as he waited for the bar to close and listened to people's

48

conversations. Finally, at 1:30 they were ushered outside with the crowd.

"Are you coming?" she asked.

"Wait, I have to ask" he said and stopped. It was cold. She was shivering waiting for him to respond. A minute or so later, he said, "Yes, it is okay, I will go with you".

Joni turned to him and said, "My son is coming in ten days. You won't be able to stay there past then."

Karl reassured, "Oh no, Samadhi is supposed to happen tonight and it shouldn't be more than ten days anyway."

Okay, she thought.

"Doesn't that make sense? It is December 12th. Of course I will be going into Samadhi on December 12th. You know, like the 12 days of Christmas."

"Okay", she said. "I guess that makes sense.

As they rode home, he told her more about Samadhi and that she would have to read about Ramakrishna and the state of Samadhi and that way she would be able to understand how to help him. During the search for him, she had gotten some books at a used book store on Jesus Christ and on schizophrenia, too. She wanted to research Jesus and other philosophical leaders so she would be able to fight "fire with fire" so to speak. She wanted to get inside his head; to talk him around to where he could get real help or perhaps come out of his delusion. There is so much to learn, and I know so little, she'd thought. She hoped she could keep astride of his knowledge and his philosophical train of thought. Somehow, I have got to listen enough, learn enough so he can trust me. We need to be on equal ground. It won't work any other way.

She resisted feeling that he might try to convert her to his philosophy and/or draw her into his own madness. She hoped that he would respect her practice.

He repeated snippets from conversations he'd heard to her as they drove along. He pieced words or phrases together that came through the airwaves to him randomly. He made divine sense out of a these 'messages' sent to him. This was not far from her own reality. So many times she had turned on her radio, passed a sign or seen some confirmation of a thought or feeling, but listening to him, she realized it was very far from her experience.

What she wanted most was to get him home safe and sound and get some rest.

She was fading fast. Most of all, she wanted to be able to report to his parents that he was safe and off the streets. She would deal with the next 24 hours in whatever way she could.

They finally made it home. There was a 'Welcome Home' sign up over her son's bedroom door which was visible as soon as they entered the apartment. She saw his eyes glance at the sign. Again, here was a sign for him; he was home. She would let him believe that 'welcome home' was for him even though he would eventually know it was for her son. Maybe it is for him though. Who knows? She handed him the wooden chalice she had wrapped in cloth. He unwrapped it. He said, "Oh, this is nice. Do you know the significance of this?"

She was excited that he had accepted the gift. "Yes, she said, I think so."
"It's the last supper", he said.

50

"Well, I really hope that your last supper will be a very long time from now, but I did want you to have this. I'm not sure where it came from." She lied. Next, she handed him a bag with the new shirt she had bought for him. She was going to give it to him for his birthday, but had decided against it. This was a perfect opportunity.

A brown print flannel, as she gave it to him, he looked at her, his eyes softening.

There was a tenderness in the way he accepted the gift that made her glad that she had given it. He thankfully took it and went to take a shower.

While he was in the shower, she called his father knowing that she would be waking him up, but not knowing how else to approach it. "Dr. Jackson, this is Joni", she said in a whisper.

"Oh, hi Joni," he groggily said.

"He's here." she whispered keeping an eye on the bathroom door. She could hear the water still running in the shower.

"I don't know what to do," Karl's father cried. "I don't know what I am going to do?"

Joni was taken aback - he's crying now? Now that I have turned myself inside out to rescue his son – now he doesn't know what to do? Her shock at his fearfulness was palpable. She needed to get off the phone – the shower was almost over.

"Well, just know that he is safe and off the streets, so you can rest easy for now. I will talk to you again soon. He's in the shower and I don't want to stay on long."

51

"Okay", he whimpered.

"God has thrown me into your arms tonight," Karl said fresh from the shower in his new shirt. "I really didn't want to go with you but He told me to." He kissed her and held her so tightly that she feared he could snap her in half with little effort, but the intensity was wonderful.

My daimoku (chanting) is what made you trust me enough to come home, she thought. *I am offering safety...that's why you're here...that may translate into God's voice in your ear, but I wonder if you could have been taken advantage of just as easily.*

She remembered her search of the past two and a half weeks...a new song had been playing on the country station...one that made her cry each time as she prayed in her own way for his safety. It went, "I believe there are angels among us, sent down to us from somewhere up above." She had hoped that an angel would find Karl, that he would be unharmed, and that somehow he would connect with someone who could help. Now it looked as though she was it, at least for the time being. She did not feel worthy or at all capable, but allowed herself to be driven by the desire to return this son safely to his parents.

During the search as she chanted she would often see a terrible scene of herself on a plane to Minneapolis escorting his dead body back. She longed to change reality to her positive dream...that of him lecturing to a large audience on how he overcame his illness. As in coma patients, she believed that there was a part of Karl that was begging the world not to give up...not to let go of the thin string that bound him to sanity.

How could she know this? No way of telling, except that she believed that she had tapped into the source of her own madness; that which is deeply imbedded in us all.

She knew instinctively that she had to keep listening to his heart. Later in explaining to friends from time to time she would tell them that she felt that no one had ever given her that gift...to never give up...to hear her heart...to understand and be patient; that's how she knew that she had to go on. For now all she could do was fall asleep.

"We'll need to go and get some food today," she said as she whipped her last three eggs into an omelet. Karl had liked the vegetable omelet she had made for him when he came home for the first night. She was happy to be able to feed him, a metaphor in her son's absence. She was working on enjoying the moment these days. That's the sum total of your life, she had read or heard somewhere...moments. They add up to your life, so not to enjoy fully was to cheat yourself out of a real life.

"So, where were you these past few weeks?" she ventured.

"I was walking the tracks to Healdsburg," he began. "God told me to. I was listening to the radio. There's this new station, the Crush...that's KRSH...Which could also be crash, but see, that's my station. Every song told me what to do. God sent me messages like do you know that song, 'Last Dance with Mary Jane'? It goes "it's the last dance with Mary Jane, one more time to end the pain..."that's about Eve."

"Who is Eve?" Joni was calculating in her head the distance between Petaluma and Healdsburg, it was over 30 miles.

"I don't think it's fair to say. She's one of the dancers, but I call her Eve. She was Eve and I was Adam in our first lives. But you know what that name means, don't you?"

53

"No, what?" Joni was fascinated by his ramblings, although she could feel her brain racing to follow his meanderings.

"Evil.", he stated. "That's where the word evil comes from."

"Anyway, then there was that other song you know it goes, "don't fall under the spell of her eyes, boy - she's not looking at you." Then just as it started to rain a song came on about being out in the rain. I got wet which was also her fault because she wouldn't give me a poncho."

"You asked her for one?" Joni didn't want to be too invasive, but wanted to grasp more firmly what had happened...if it was at all possible.

"Yes. And I asked her to come and pick me up but she said 'no'. I couldn't believe it!

She knew for a whole year who I was. She knew. I told her everything and if she had thought about it for five seconds she would have known what I'm going to be like after Samadhi. Just five seconds! I couldn't believe she wouldn't help me. But God told me on my walk that if I had married her it wouldn't have been good anyway. She would have taken too much attention away. She's really evil, anyway."

"Maybe she didn't understand," Joni was tenuous, "maybe she didn't realize that you were in love with her. Did you tell her?"

He hesitated. Joni knew it was time to wait out his silence once again. The sum total of their silences was definitely greater than that of their speaking moments.

54

"I wasn't in love with her," he faltered as if that hadn't occurred to him before, but now he was analyzing the thought as he stared at his plate. "I wanted to tell her beautiful things from God. So many wonderful, beautiful things. But she just yelled at me."

Some time went by as they both ate in silence. Then Karl picked up the conversation as if he'd been given a celestial go ahead.

"I get points for telling you this. Before it was better not to say anything, but God says it's okay for me to tell you these things and it's really helping me."

"I'm glad you can talk to me, Karl. I want to help you. I'm sorry that things didn't work out for you and Eve. Is that why you left?"

"I told you I was doing what God said. It wasn't because of Eve, you need to pay attention and besides, God said, 'you didn't lose your temper, did you? You didn't even raise your voice the whole time she was yelling at you, did you? So I knew I had done the right thing."

"Didn't you go to San Francisco, too, Karl?"

Another pause and then a shake of the head. "No."

"What did you eat when you were walking?" Joni wanted to get back to more concrete issues.

"Cheetos!" exclaimed Karl. "See, I saw a sign on a truck that said, 'Cheetos Are Good Food' so I got Cheetos. That's what God wanted me to eat. I walked and walked, but I finally couldn't walk anymore and I fell asleep and then got rained on."

"It's amazing you didn't get sick out in the cold and rain like that," Joni was gentle and warm in her tone. "I've got to do morning prayers and then we can go to the store and get whatever food you like."

Joni did the dishes then got in front of her altar as she did each morning and evening. Her prayer this morning was to touch Karl's heart. To help him to feel safe enough to ask for help to have the space and comfort to get well. Most of all she chanted for his true happiness...whatever form that took.

"Wayne, will you write a 'To Whom It May Concern' letter for Karl's parents? They need to prove he needs help. Just in case they have to commit him."

"No way," he answered. "That is interfering with his free will."

"I know, but what if his free will is keeping him from living the life he really wants?

What if his free will means that he dies in the streets before he's 40?" Joni was not 100% sold on the idea of commitment, either, but she didn't know what else to do with Karl's parents' request.

"I had another friend in a similar situation," Wayne went on. "They locked him up and he took his first opportunity to commit suicide. So, getting him off the street was his death sentence, I always wonder to this day, if I had left well enough alone if he would have survived."

Joni was grateful for Wayne's opposing opinion. It leant balance to the equation even though it made all thought circle back on itself in a Mobius strip. No amount of posturing or mental figuring was going to get her through this situation.   Mr.

Nagashima's advice echoed through her heart's chambers. "Chant and follow your wisdom."

Karl walked by quietly as Joni chanted. He was visibly respectful of her time and intent in her prayers. As she ended and was closing up her butsadon that housed her scroll (Gohonzon) he came by smiling and eating an apple.

"God's impressed with your prayers." His voice was quiet, but filled with command.

Joni beamed, "Thank you," she said. She was thankful for Karl's sincerity and respectful nature. It had taken her a full 45 minutes to complete...and some days she would chant longer.

"Let's go!" She was feeling positive and happy; no worry about the fact that she barely had enough money to cover the food bill. Somehow she would make it. This man needs food, she thought. This is no time to worry about money.

At the store she picked out vegetables and fruits. "Do you like oranges?" A shy nod was his response. "Why don't you pick out a loaf of bread?"

Complying quietly, hesitantly, he would return to the cart holding an item as if it were precious and undeserved. He looked at her with eyes that searched for a false move, not suspiciously, just wonderment at how this was happening to him.

"Can you think of anything else you'd like?" she'd ask.

"That's fine." he said shaking his head no. Then with a laugh, "You've got to remember I've been living on Cheetos for the last two and a half weeks..."

57

"Do you want to get some Cheetos?" she wise-assed back, chuckling.

"No", he laughed.

This is hopeful, thought Joni...*he remembers clearly the events of the past few weeks. He's not altering what he says, so maybe his brain isn't too far gone. If he can feel safe for long enough, maybe he can get well.* She desperately wanted to know more about psychology. She had taken stolen moments on lunch hours and in front of her altar while chanting to read parts of her book on schizophrenia. "It should always be remembered that the behavior of schizophrenic persons is internally logical and rational; they do things for reasons which, given their disordered senses and thinking, make sense to them. To the outside observer the behavior may appear irrational, "crazy," "mad," the very hallmark of the disease. To the schizophrenic person, however, there is nothing "crazy" or "mad" about it at all."

That night they shared a dinner of vegetables and tea. Joni didn't mind cooking vegetarian for him. She looked on it as a new challenge and a healthy one at that. After dinner Karl showered.

"My foot is a little sore," he suggested.

Joni had commented earlier that he seemed to be walking as if his feet hurt. He was fine he had calmly assured her. Now as he sat on the bed in his freshly cleaned pants, bare-chested and twisting his foot up and across his other knee, he welcomed her attention.

"Oh, Karl..." Joni was shocked..."you're bleeding. That must really hurt..."His foot was cracked and calloused and bleeding from rivulets carved in broken skin.

"It's from my feet getting wet and then drying that way. They got wet out in the rain and I didn't have any extra shoes..."

"This should help," Joni spoke softly as she took his large foot in her hands and kneeling beside him rubbed vitamin E oil gently into the soles.

"Does that hurt at all?" she asked.

Karl shook his head no. As she oiled his foot gently and lovingly she was aware of his tender look. *Here I am rubbing Jesus' feet...I know that's what he's thinking, she thought. Well, there's Jesus in all of us...*her mind continued as she rubbed the oil into his other foot. *We call it the Buddha nature - same thing.* It felt wonderful to be able to help him heal. As she worked she imagined healing going throughout his body and mind...her Buddha nature spoke to his in the non-language of sincere respect. We're all worthy of that. Inside she cried at the thought of how alone he must have felt out in the rain, on the tracks in the dark.

"That's fine, "he said quietly. He seemed mildly embarrassed at having allowed this sensual experience.

"Let me take a look at them again tomorrow or so," she said matter-of-factly. "I'll leave this oil out for you, too." Changing the subject, "Do you want to watch a movie?"

"What do you have?" Karl asked eyeing the collection of videos Joni had amassed over the years. Then he stopped and suggested Joni choose. It was getting confusing for him to read the titles.

"How about a comedy?" she asked - knowing that he hadn't been very interested in comedies the last time she saw him, but hoping to nudge him in that direction. "It's mostly what

I have," she offered. "I know one you might enjoy...'Ferris Beuller's Day Off', it's one of my all-time favorites!"

Her enthusiasm carried the vote. 'Ferris Beuller' won and Karl was not at all disappointed. Joni delighted that he laughed at the appropriate places and seemed to really enjoy the experience keeping her in his arms as they watched from the bed.

Afterward some kisses in the dark and tender wrestling gave way to peaceful sleep despite the ivy-cling to one another.

He drew a line that shut me out.-
Heretic, rebel, a thing to flout.
But Love and I had the wit to win:
We drew a circle that took him in!

-       Edwin Markham

Chapter Four   The Taming

"I haven't felt this rested in a very long time," Karl smiled from his propped-up position in the bed. Joni had just come out of the shower and was putting the finishing touches on to her workday outfit.

"I'm glad, "she answered. "You said you wanted to go to the mall? I can drop you off on my way in to work. How about some breakfast before I start gongyo?"

"Sure," he said, moving toward the shower. "I won't take too long."

Joni launched into preparations. Tea and English muffins with jam and cream cheese. Hoping it would be, she made a lunch for him to take along also.   *This   is strange*, she thought. *I'm really enjoying having him here. In fact, it feels so natural. We are getting along so well, but*

61

maybe it will change...anyway, I've told him that Kevin is coming in ten days, so he'll have to be gone by then.

She chose from her assortment of teas and neatly placed the pot on the table nearest to his place.

"I hope you like this kind," she said pouring the tea. "There is cream cheese here, too and some homemade jam...it's been around a while, though.

Karl ate politely, gingerly and said little. Joni ate, too, although her morning routine up until this time had involved a drive-through somewhere fast on her way to work. I may actually save money by eating at home, too she thought. This may be a little nudge to change my ways and teach me how to better care for myself. Interesting!

"God wants me to listen again today, "Karl offered. "Actually the people in the mall are the most spiritual people on earth right now, but they don't know it."

Joni continued eating through the lapses into silence.

"Easwaran, that's my guru, he thinks he's so spiritual, but he really isn't. He didn't even recognize me! It's his job to help me to prepare for Samadhi, but he hasn't done one thing to help me."

"Oftentimes people who appear to be spiritual really aren't, "Joni wanted to keep communication open and she believed sincerely in what she was saying.

"I need to start gongyo now, we can leave right after that." Once again she prayed for wisdom and Karl's health. She prayed for her son's safe flight and enjoyable visit.

She prayed to fulfill her mission - whatever it might be - in this time and in this place and in this family. He's so smart, she thought, I hope he grasps the validity of this practice and becomes a great leader for world peace in reality! He is a good, good man. He has to be able to reach for help.

Joni dropped him off at the mall for his day and drive on to her office to start her own. Shortly after she got settled at her desk the phone rang.

"Can you meet me for lunch?" Chris's voice sounded more like a plea than a question.

"Okay, "agreed Joni. She owed him at least that much. She would explain to him again that she had to do whatever it was she had to do with Karl for now. She would say quite honestly that she didn't know how long this would last or what exactly would happen, but that she didn't intend to give up dancing. For now, though, and for the week during Kevin's visit, she had more than enough to think about.

"I feel like you dumped me for Karl," he stated clearly. "I don't understand why we can't still see each other. You said we could have three months."

"I'm sorry. I know, but things are different now. You must understand, Chris...I was talking about Life 101, not a relationship, as you recall. It was a mistake."

"That's just the point!" Chris argued. He shook his head fervently. His voice rose to a controlled yell, "No! I think what happened was just a natural progression from spending so much time together. I don't feel like it was a mistake at all."

Joni sighed and her eyes searched the table for an answer, "I'm sorry, but I can only be with one man at a time. Karl was in the picture well before you ever were. I feel that I owe him a karmic debt. I know you don't understand that, but this is really powerful for me. This whole thing with Karl has been powerful from the beginning." She didn't let on that there was nothing sexual between her and Karl –

"All right, I don't understand about karma and the way your belief system works, but I feel that you're an important person for me. I don't want to just be dumped."

"Chris, I really do understand what you're saying, but I never intended for this to be a relationship other than a friendship. I'm sorry for hurting you. I really am. You are a good friend, and I don't think that has to end, but if it's too painful for you, then I absolutely understand. I won't ask you to dance from now on, I'll wait until you ask me - so that I know you're comfortable. Other than that, I can't do anything else. Karl is in my house. That's the reality for now and if that means I've ruined our friendship, too...I'm sorry, but I have no other choice right now."

As Joni drove back to work she felt sad at the thought of Chris's pain. How she wished she had not given in to 'the experiment' quite so soon. It was only 24 hours later that Karl was there.

"Hi Joni," said Karl brightly as she approached her car.

"Karl!" she smiled. "How did you find me?"

"I saw your car," he answered.

She had given him her business card that morning in case he wanted to call. She would pick him up at the mall after work, but now he had gotten all the way across town to her office and was ready to leave for home with her.

How considerate and independent he is...he found the place, got himself here and all at the right time...he has a better sense of time and responsibility than most men I know! He also called me by name - so many men friends fail to do that - they substitute a generic "hon" or "babe". He's definitely on my wavelength!

"How was your day?" Joni asked as they drove home.

"Fine." he answered quietly. His usual silence ensued.

Joni was growing used to it. In some ways it was familiar. She, too, needed time to think and process...more-so than most other people she knew. It may have given the appearance of stupidity, but her slow manner was filled with non-verbal calculation. She instinctively knew that he was in that place beyond words.

Home again she muttered under her breath as they parked in the driveway. Karl wasn't talking. A depressive something-or-other seemed to be lurking around him, maybe within him. A cloud, perhaps, that he could walk through if he smiled. But no smile was forthcoming. He entered the house and immediately sat down in one of the two oversized easy chairs.

"Are you hungry?" she asked running her hand along his shoulder gently.

"Leave me alone," he sneered. He closed his eyes to shut her out.

"It's okay if you want to meditate for a while, she said. "I'll do my prayers...if it won't disturb you."

"No, that would be okay," his tone softer now, almost embarrassed.

As she chanted she prayed for him. He must feel strange here in this warm home after having been on the street so long, she thought. Please let my heart speak to his. Let him know that he's safe. Let him want to come back to a full life. Let him want to get well. Let him want to return to his family.

She cooked dinner in silence; sending out healing energy and love as she moved around the kitchen. She could feel his confusion and his pain and her mind raced to keep up with her telepathy. He needs to feel my caring in that place where he is beyond words. *Don't talk too much*, she thought.

As they sat at the table Karl ate quietly, but was fidgety and agitated. "It must be difficult for you to be here," she ventured. No sound.

Let it be, she admonished herself silently. *Let it be. You must learn patience.*

"He didn't even know that I was Ramakrishna! He was always talking about non- violence and he couldn't see that I did a perfectly non-violent act against him by working."

"You mean Easwaran?"

"Yeah. It's like there he is - being carried off the ashram. There he is - getting kicked out of his apartment. There he is - carrying his stuff down the street. There he is

- stealing groceries."

Joni was more than tuned in to his pain and disbelief. "How did this happen?" was written in the air between them. And the void of no answer was simultaneously understood. She sighed when there was air enough, and looked at him tenderly.

"You've really been through it, haven't you?"

His head had been jerking as he remembered these scenes. The anger underlying his disbelief was salient. He looked at her now as if she might be responsible for all that had gone before in his life. His contempt for her nurturing burst forth, "Some people just want to be appreciated." He was condescending and accusatory.

Joni spoke slowly and quietly after searching herself for the truth. "You're right," she said. "I think that most people do want to be appreciated. I enjoy that feeling."

Tension diffused. Culpability shared. Acceptance. Safety. Healing.

"Do you want to go for a walk?" Karl asked sweetly.

"Sure!" Joni responded. "Just let me get the dishes done and I'll be ready."

On their walk Karl held her hand. She listened when he talked and she listened when he was silent. *I need to learn, to know him*, she felt. *I have to be one step ahead of him to help him to wellness. I wish I knew more philosophy. He's so brilliant, he won't tolerate stupidity or bull...he'll see right through me if I try to fake it. My only hope is to be sincere and strong.*

That night they slept well again, but only after passionate kissing and wrestling. His hands never went below her waist.

"Not down there," he'd priss if her touch got too close to his underwear. Maybe it was because it had been so long since she had had a sexual relationship, or maybe it was because of the depth of connection she felt with him...whatever the reason, Joni was orgasmic. This has never happened to her this way. It wasn't sex she'd been missing...but intimacy. Of course, sex would be nice, too, but she could be patient with that one. She wanted to explore whatever it was.

The next morning came quickly after a restful sleep.

"God wants me to rejoin the community," Karl said softly holding Joni's freshly showered and dressed body close. They were lying on the bed. He had pulled her down on top of him and kissed her gently.

"You mean go back out on the street?" Joni was incredulous.

"That's what He says, and I have to do what He says."

"Where will you sleep?" she asked stupidly.

Silence. *Dumb question*, she thought. *There is no answer for it...he'll sleep wherever he's been sleeping for the past year.*

Hot tears welled up in her eyes and cautiously began their descent to his chest below.

"I'll take my shower now," he said heaving her up gently.

"Wait," she demanded with firm vulnerability. "I'm having trouble with this..." she tried to hold her sobs back. He laid back down carefully, to hear her out. His uncertainty held stiffly in his chest was balanced by the tenderness that wouldn't shake from his arms and fingertips.

"Does God love me?" She softly asked through her tears. Her thought processes had shut down; she could only say what came out of her mouth not knowing what to think or do.

"God loves everyone."

Perfect answer she thought. *Straight out of catechism class...of course that was his only possible answer...ask - ask what you really want to know.*

"What about Karl? Who does Karl love?" No response....

"If you have to go, I can't stop you, but I love you, Karl Jackson. And no matter where you go, no matter how far you run you won't ever change that. I've seen the beautiful man inside and I have been with him. My heart is always open."

She released him and he headed for the shower. She put breakfast on the table and then knelt before her altar. Be strong, she prayed to herself. Don't make a scene. If he's meant to go, you cannot hold him. You've done all you can.

At breakfast she decided to read to him from her Buddhist newspaper, The World Tribune. He was happy to hear about her religion, so she shared some paragraphs she hoped would reach his heart.

"Showing deep sensitivity ...the Daishonin writes (to a follower):

Even though I cannot see you, I am convinced that your heart remains here with me... Whenever you yearn for me, Nichiren, look toward the sun which rises in the morning and the moon which appears in the evening. I will invariably be reflected in the sun and the moon. In the next life, let us meet in the pure land of Eagle Peak. (The Major Writings of Nichiren Daishonin, vol.4, p.142)

"Even if we cannot meet personally, I am always by your side. (President Ikeda followed.) I will be reflected in the sun and the moon and watch over you without fail.

We will be together eternally." This is the spirit if the original Buddha, Nichiren Daishonin, and the quintessence of the Daishonin's Buddhism."

With that she fought back a tear, but kept her promise to herself not to cry.

"If I've made a mistake, I'll call you," he said as they headed for the car. She wasn't sure of his look...was it doubt or a masking of intense relief?

Keep your head up, she thought. *You don't own him and he doesn't owe you a thing. This may be a protection from the Buddhist gods...there will be an answer in time. And why in the world did you tell him that you loved him? It's a good thing this is over.*

"Will you call me sometime just to let me know that you're alive?" She nudged.

They were nearing the drop-off point where he would walk out of her life.

He nodded. Then with a quick peck on the lips he jumped out at the corner. "Have a good day," she tried to be cheerful. His eyes looked heavy in their sockets, his words didn't form in time - he was on the street again.

At least he has some food with him she thought. That will last a day or two. What am I going to tell his parents? Joni felt a heaviness that seemed to stretch back through past lifetimes. This lesson is one I need to finish learning, she thought. This is just too painful. It's okay to cry she told her tears.

Maybe he'll call later. If not, I'll call his folks when I get home.

The day steamrollered down the minutes into hours. No word. Let the time pass, she thought. Let it go. It's for the best. But her fear for his life would not subside. It's his choice now. Maybe this is what he truly wants or needs. Maybe he's too far gone. Most men do seem to go running away screaming...men supposedly far healthier. But this isn't about me, it's about facing up to needing help. It's about feeling and living through the pain when you can't outrun it any longer.

"Hi Donald, its Joni."

"Elaine, its Joni! Get on the other phone!"

"Hi Joni," Elaine was expectant, too.

"I know it's early, but I thought I should call this morning before work...Karl has gone back out on the street." her voice broke.

"He's back out, Elaine," Donald said "Where is he going to go? Where is he now? What happened?"

"He told me that God wanted him to 'rejoin the community'..."

"Rejoin the community? That means live on the street?" queried Donald.

"Oh, no..." Elaine was sobbing on the other line.

"I can't look for him anymore," cried Joni. "I told him that he's welcome to come back. I told him that I loved him and that my heart was always open, but I can't look for him anymore."

"Oh, no, no..." said Elaine between tears. "It just breaks your heart doesn't it?"

"This has to come to an end," said Donald in a distressed tone. "I don't know how much more of this we can take. One way or another, this has to end."

"He said he would call if he made a mistake, but I know he doesn't ever admit to making mistakes."

73

"No, Karl wouldn't ever say he made a mistake. It's not in his pattern, at all. He left Corrine, too. He had only been there about two weeks and she wanted him to contribute in some way. She wasn't asking for anything unreasonable, but he couldn't take her demands on him."

"I've been very careful, "Joni said mildly defensively. "I have been trying to make him feel safe enough to sleep and to eat and see what affect that would have on his mental state. I haven't made any demands on him at all. I know he's also dealing with the adjustment to just living with another person at this stage...he may be back...he knows my work number and my home number...."

"I thought we were making progress because he was sleeping," said Donald. "What will you do if he calls?"

"If he calls, he can come back. I'll let you know immediately."

" You won't tell him you've talked to us?" questioned Donald..."I don't think that would go over well."

"No, right now I think it's better not to."

"Well, call us if you hear anything..." started Elaine. "You've handled this beautifully. And he might come back."

"If he does come back now, I feel that it will be a move toward health for him. It has to be his decision, though."

74

They all agreed.

"I'm praying for a complete miracle, "said Elaine. "And this is just the start of it." "Me, too," said Joni. "I'll let you know what happens."

That night Joni went dancing half hoping that Karl would be there. He wasn't. Is Karl back out on the street?" Wayne asked her during a break.

"Yes," said Joni, "right now I feel that if he comes back, I'll take him back, but I don't really think he will. My karma with him may be complete. I feel like I've done all that I can do."

"Well that's healthy." Wayne understood much about karma, and metaphysics, but he was also well balance and intelligent. He was genuinely interested in Joni's as well as Karl's wellbeing.

Joni chanted the half hour drive home as she always did. The radio played in the background, "I believe there are angels among us, sent down to us from somewhere up above...to show us how to live, teach us how to give..." she cried again. Why does everything have to get so complicated? She thought. Why don't I just find this perfect man that everyone seems to think is out there for me? If I did, would he understand this necessity I have to be there for Karl? Nam myoho renge kyo. Nam myoho renge kyo.

Nam myoho renge kyo.

It was Wednesday morning. Joni had to go to work and face the day at work. She had hired her mother almost five years earlier. Isabel had worked out beautifully as an office

75

assistant and had much better organizational skills than Joni. With the role reversal of daughter as boss of mother they had both felt some trepidation at the start, but a new respect had formed for each other through the years. Isabel saw Joni as the capable, adult assistant to a high-powered doctor/public speaker - no longer just her little girl or her rebellious non-conformist teenaged nightmare. Joni saw her mother as a skillful organizer and her never-complaining attitude was a breath of fresh air after past co-workers. They had days when there was minor tension - mainly build-up of too much togetherness for Joni. She felt that way with everyone at one time or another. But, there were other days when their rhythms meshed completely - work was done – or conversations about the family mingled with the slower work days or jokes were told until they both cried and gasped for air. It was usually Isabel who could pull it together to answer the phone during these sessions, Joni was usually too far gone into hysteria. And during those times especially, Joni savored those moments with her mother.

Shared time that could never have been planned. Real time - real appreciation for the laughter that only deeply bonded people share. Someday this will be over...the thought would streak across her mind. Enjoy it now.

Today though, she was dreading the inevitable. To tell her mother that Karl was gone...to hear the relief in her mother's voice...to quietly state both truths: That she wouldn't be looking for him, but that he was welcomed to come back...and that either way it was okay...but how her mood felt sad.

"You can't run someone else's life, "said Isabel. "You've already learned that with Eddie. Some people just want to live that way."

"I know, "Joni would said as little as possible and tried to stay open at the same time.

It was days like these that working with her mother felt unnatural. It was bad enough that they lived in the same house, but worked at respecting each other's space and time...at work there was no escape. Conversations were hard to hear. Joni was always measuring how much to share and where to draw the line. At times she would say, "You're my co-worker now, not my mother..."as a preface to some secret. They both held it all in good humor, but it wasn't always easy.

After lunch Joni was feeling extremely tired as she did sometimes in the afternoon.

Depression in small measure.

"I'm going to take a nap," she said to Isabel.

"Fine, go ahead, I'll call the answering service, "said Isabel cheerfully.

Joni could always count on her to cover...and fifteen minutes of rest would make a huge difference in her attitude most days.

The door to the dark exam room slid open almost as soon as Joni closed it. In the wedge of bright office light, Isabel stood smiling with fists in goodie-goodie childlike motion at her chest. "Karl from Coddingtown called! The service said he said he'd call back at two...I figured you'd want to be woken up for that!" She smiled supportively.

"Karl! Yes, thank you!"

Joni flew off the exam table where she had planned to rest. Her heart was pounding now. Adrenaline had erased all feelings of fatigue. "What if he doesn't call back?"

"The service said that he said he'd call back..."

"If he doesn't call back maybe I'll go to Coddingtown after work." Joni was in overdrive.

"He'll call." Her mother assured her.

Coddingtown was a shopping mall in Santa Rosa. How clever that he said he was from Coddingtown, she thought.

Sure enough just a few minutes after two the phone rang. Joni answered with her heart in her mouth.

"Hi, Joni? It's Karl."

"Oh, Karl, hi. How are you?" She had never talked to him on the phone before. He sounded so young and happy - as if his voice didn't really fit his body when you saw him in person.

"It seems I made a mistake," he went on. "I'm supposed to be with you."

"You are?" Joni was excited, "What do you want me to do? Should I pick you up somewhere after work?"

"I'll meet you at your office," ventured Karl.

"Okay, that's fine."

"Great!" he quipped. Joni was amazed at the lightness of his voice and humor. He said great...I can't believe he used that word.

Immediately she picked up the phone and called Elaine and Donald.

"Karl just called! He's coming back with me tonight. He sounded happy...said he made a mistake!"

"I can't believe it! That's wonderful! It's not like Karl to say he's made a mistake...let's see how this goes and, Joni, I'm going to send you a check to help pay for some of your expenses and for Karl's food, etc. You must have spent some money trying to find him and all and we really appreciate it."

"That's okay, "Joni replied. "It isn't necessary. I did spend some money, but that's not why I'm doing this..."

"We know you haven't asked, but we do appreciate your help."

"Thank you, that's very nice of you." she felt humble, but also grateful for the help that she would never have asked for. Her philosophy was that it would all work out...but money was very tight, so to completely refuse the help wasn't practical either.

"I'll let you know how it goes, " Joni was wrapping up the conversation too excited about seeing Karl and his condition to think of much else or to talk.

Elaine was on the phone now, too. "We're still praying for him, Joni. We'll be in touch. Thank you so much for what you are doing! You're an angel!"

"Oh, no," said Joni, "but I appreciate your support. Thank you. We'll talk soon. Bye."

As Joni walked out of her office that night she expected to see Karl waiting there.

He wasn't. What now? She thought...did he change his mind? Well, I can't wait all night. He's got fifteen minutes, then I just leave...and I'm not looking for him. She no sooner got through this thought process than she saw him coming across the parking lot. Relief swept through her body.

80

"Hi, Joni!," he smiled his usual underplayed smile and kissed her as he approached. "Sorry I'm late."

"Well, it's only a few minutes after five," she reassured him. She felt taken aback, but that was mild compared to the next wave of emotion that would sweep her....

As they got into the car, Karl looked at her directly and smiled the biggest smile she had ever seen him attempt. "I love you, too," he looked her straight in the eyes. "I thought so, but I had to be sure. God says it's all going to be okay, too...we can get married and have sex and everything...right after I go into Samadhi. You're supposed to help me and after that I'll teach and then it may also be that I'll help you go into Samadhi, too."

"I'm glad," was all Joni could muster cheerfully. *Whoa, boy!,* she thought. *How did we get to marriage? This is bizarre! He is so sincere, I need to let him feel safe and not challenge this now. Perhaps it's a passing feeling, anyway. At least he's chosen to come back of his own free will. It's a positive sign that he wants to connect...I hope.*

"I'm supposed to be on the cover of Time magazine, too." Karl explained as Joni drove. "You are going to be there with me, too."

"I'm definitely not interested in being famous," she cautioned, "I really just want to support you and stay in the background on this."

81

How do I get around this stuff, she thought. *What do I say? I don't want to alienate him, but I don't want to completely go along with his delusions, either. He may very well be on the cover of Time at some point, but probably not for the reasons he thinks.*

Maybe he'll make a great contribution to the field of psychology someday...or maybe in a scientific field. The possibilities are endless. I know that there is a wealth of capability and accomplishment locked up inside this man. How does one approach this? Who would agree that they are mentally ill when that is their only frame of reference? It would be like denouncing one's own personality, perhaps...or like deciding that up was now down. Her brain contorted with the permutations. And then the ultimate question...was it right to 'help' someone who didn't seek help?

In caring for a child one often has to control their impulses that are destructive...for their own good. This man was not a child...or was he? Joni hated and loved herself simultaneously for having such an analytical side. More than once in life she had thought herself through mazes and loops and whirls and into corners. Sometimes it was a strength; sometimes a royal pain in the ass. She wasn't sure which right now, but it didn't feel real comfortable.

"I have to go to a meeting tonight, would you like to come?"

Karl nodded with enthusiasm, "Yes. I should be able to get some messages there."

I hope he doesn't announce that he's Jesus Christ tonight, but if he does, we'll deal with it. There is no place safer or more accepting on earth than a Buddhist meeting.

What a great benefit it would be if he could connect with some of the men! I'll take my chances...after all, what choice do I really have? There is no easy solution to this problem...but anything is possible through Buddhism!

During gongyo she tried to run her finger underneath each of the phonetic Japanese words so that he could follow along. Seconds into it, though, he shook his head annoyed by the practice. He closed his eyes and meditated to the sound of the rhythmical chanting. Fine, she thought. It's okay. It will take time. He will soak in the daimoku just being here, anyway. He's already made a tremendous cause by coming along.

She envisioned the future as she chanted...how at that time he would stand up and give an experience of how the practice helped him overcome schizophrenia and how his life had changed so dramatically. It wasn't so far-fetched a dream at all. Don Ross had done just that!

I'll need to call Don, she thought. He'll know how I should approach this in terms of faith based on his own experience. Don had recently given an experience at a large meeting about how he had changed and about the challenges he was still facing. Joni had joined shortly before Don had. She vividly remembered how off the wall he had been. He had worn bandannas on his head with earrings and large clunky crosses around his neck. He seemed to always be on drugs and had euphoric episodes that no one else seemed to be able to relate to. Still, she had liked him even then, but when it had been announced that he had discovered he was HIV positive she had been saddened beyond words. In the year that

83

followed she had developed an unspoken and deeply held respect for him as she heard that he was chanting 8 hours a day for his life. He wasn't able to come out to meetings, because at that time no one really knew for sure how AIDS was transmitted and the organization felt it prudent to keep him separated. He had, however, been granted special permission to attend her wedding and she had been thrilled to have him participate.

"Kiss me," he said as she walked in to the temple in her wedding dress. She remembered swallowing her fear as she kissed him. Will I get AIDS? Is this worth it? It's too late to worry about it now...simultaneously a scene from the movie, 'Papillon' ran through her mind. The head leper of the colony where Papy landed in his escape had offered him the cigar from his own disfigured lips. Papillon had taken it and out of respect puffed on it. The leper roared with laughter..."How did you know that I have dry leprosy? That it is not contagious?" he wailed. "I didn't" was Papillon's response. She moved quickly realizing the pain her hesitation could cause. She had kissed him and was heartened by his beaming smile. Now, seven years later, she was glad she did.

Don was a beacon of hope for her - that perhaps there was still time for Karl to realize his highest potential in life. She wanted desperately for the two men to connect, but it was not to be. Karl sat quietly through the meeting and afterward Tom, who had practiced for almost 20 years spoke with him. Joni had already briefed Tom that she was bringing a guest to the meeting and Tom and his wife, Robbie, were among the few people who knew the full story of her search for Karl. Joni was impressed all over again with Tom's compassionate, gentle attitude toward Karl. He openly shared with Karl his dream of living totally on the proceeds of his art work which hung in the house. He had recently left his job with disturbed teenagers

84

after serving 8 years, and was pursuing his dream. Karl seemed happy to be able to share in Tom's life, but there was no real connection.

"God said that Tom was one of my disciples when I was Ramakrishna," said Karl on the drive home.

"Really?" asked Joni trying to be open minded, or at least keep up the appearance of such. She was tired. She longed for real conversation. She wanted to tell him that although his feelings could be correct, there was little value in just stating past-life connections without any practical purpose in present life. It was all well and good that we are reincarnated with persons from past lives, but the key is in how we handle those relationships; how we grow from the seed of that understanding; how we create value with that knowledge. Instead, she just bit her tongue and opened her heart and mind a tiny crack beyond the point of comfort. "That's really interesting. We do believe that we have all been together in past lives."

Karl shrugged. He was uncomfortable with Joni's chatter. He didn't want to listen; he wanted to speak. He was frustrated by the lack of speed with which his words were spoken. He wanted to best her with his wit. He wanted her to understand that he was a superior being. He turned up the radio to drown out the possibility that she would speak again, even though she had only spoken two sentences - they grated on him. He had long lost his ease with lengthy conversation. Inside the music once again, he felt calm and focused. The distraction helped him become aware again of his attraction to Joni. He quietly wedged his elbow shoulder high between the bucket seats so that his hand draped down barely touching her shoulder as she drove. He sensed her awareness of his dilemma and her acceptance. He felt almost safe.

From what she could discern he was a pretty much classic case. But his super intelligence made it difficult to hoodwink him into even a net of his own making. He clearly wasn't going to fall for her original idea of telling him that his disciples were gathering in Minneapolis. She'd take it one day at a time.

"I'm having some women over on Saturday night," Joni was cautioning Karl. She didn't quite know how to handle the situation. She had planned a birthday party for her friend, Shirlee, months ago. She wasn't about to cancel it now…but she didn't want to include Karl in the all-woman event, either. "It's a birthday party for my friend, Shirlee, because she never gets parties since her birthday is so close to Christmas."

"That's fine," said Karl cheerfully. "I'll just walk home from the bus stop."

"Oh, that part is okay," Joni was handling this gingerly, "I can pick you up at the bus stop, I just wanted to let you know that it wouldn't be a regular day - and I have no real control over what time everyone will leave and stuff. Do you think you could amuse yourself by watching a movie or something?"

"That's no problem," Karl assured her.

Saturday rolled around in no time at all and Karl went off to spend the day at the mall. He would return to town on the 7 o'clock bus and Joni would pick him up there.

86

The party got underway in late afternoon and Joni was enjoying it immensely. All of the women were supposed to wear hats and they came in a wide variety of types and colors. It was a small group, seven in all, with Shirlee's friend, Cheryl, arriving last.

When she arrived the party began its second wind. She was quite vivacious and fun. Joni's mother had pitched in and made a wonderful batch of her famous brandy slush and everyone was raving about it and asking for the recipe. A frozen concoction mixed with 7-UP, it was a very drinkable libation. The brandy part sneaks up on you quietly.

It was fun for Joni to be doing something social with friends and even though she didn't know a couple of Shirlee's friends that well, she felt she could be herself. But, the moment of truth was fast approaching. She was going to have to leave and pick Karl up. She wished she hadn't said she'd pick him up. It wasn't raining as reports had predicted, but there was no way of contacting him now. The party was just getting warmed up - so there was no chance at all that it would break up in time for her to get off without explanation. She chose the bold approach that she usually reserved for such occasions as this.

"Well, got to go pick up Jesus," she announced as she got up to get her coat and car keys. "I'll be right back, just need to pick him up at the shopping center in town."

The girls looked at each other. "Jesus?" The ones who knew giggled nervously and Shirlee started to explain to her friends about the homeless man who was living with Joni. She looked up with a "help me!" look as she spoke, "His name is Kirk? Isn't it?"

"Karl," said Joni with very little of the apology one might expect in this situation. "He just thinks he's Jesus. But, he's really harmless." She added the second part in response to the fearful faces now surrounding her closer friends. "I'm just keeping him off the streets until his parents can come and get him or something." She was halfway out the door now. "I'll be back in 15 minutes!" she chirped as she slid the door closed behind her. She could only imagine the conversations flying back and forth as she drove away, knowing that as she re-entered the house, all would go silent again. She had felt bad in part for being so flippant about Karl's condition, but she felt it was best to bring it up before she walked in with him - just in case he started spouting off. She wasn't quite sure what he would do - and she feared a worse scene than the one she had just created. She had visions of everyone in the party getting up and leaving in droves before she returned, but she was pleasantly surprised to see them all warm and cozy by the fire when she returned.

"Everyone, this is Karl Jackson," she said as they came through the door. Then she named off to Karl each woman in turn so that they could say hello. After the initial intro she followed Karl into the kitchen and gave him a plate and some brandy slush. "You might as well get drunk, too," she joked as he took a sip to try it out. "You're welcomed to join us after you eat, or you can have the TV or whatever," she said.

"Sure, come and talk with us," a couple of the girls said. Their curiosity peaked as well. But Karl was not about to join in. He decided that he needed to meditate and retired after quietly saying how nice it was to have met everyone. Had Joni not spoken ahead of time, they probably would never have known that he was off balance.

The party went on and jokes flew fast and furiously. There were bursts of uproarious laughter followed by oos and aahs as Joni read each person's fortune in turn. Toward the end of the circle of readings, everyone seemed to sense that it was time to go.

They called out good-byes to Karl as they left, but got no response. 'Maybe he's sleeping," one woman said in almost a whisper. After that everyone was whispering their goodbyes and tiptoeing out as they left. It was a great success - and colorful to say the least, but Joni had even greater feelings of respect and admiration for the women who had so graciously accepted the predicament they were in. Not one of them ever came back to her with a complaint or criticism of her behavior, and though they might never know it, Joni would always deeply appreciate their generosity.

"Love is an act of endless forgiveness, a tender look which becomes a habit."

- Peter Ustinov

Chapter Five   - Torn

"I'm not sure what to do," Joni was on the phone again with Elaine and Donald. "I don't think he'll come home and I hate to send him out on the street again, but my son is coming next week."

"I'd hate for him to go out again after we've made all of this progress." Donald was stressed. "Isn't there some chance that he'll come home...even if we just say it's for a visit?"

"He doesn't seem to want to discuss it, and don't want to push him at this point. I've told him that my son is coming and that he's welcome to be here for Christmas day and dinner, etc. I just don't know if he'll take off again."

"Your son comes first," Elaine stated flatly. "He doesn't need to have a ding-a-ling around for his Christmas. Karl will just have to go."

"Maybe he would be good with your son, though." Donald was pulling at straws. "Maybe it would help him to come out of it. Maybe there's something he could help your son with?"

"I just don't know," hesitated Joni, "But, I'll do my best. If worst came to worst I know I could find him again." The words rolled out of her mouth like leaden boulders. The thought of starting from that point all over again was heavy and slowed her breathing.

"I'm really afraid that he would get worse. I know he wouldn't sleep..." Donald rolled the boulders back at her.

"I'm going to pray for a complete miracle," Elaine lightened, "now that we've come this far he just has to get better!"

"Yes, Elaine," Joni replied, "I'm praying, too. Between the two of us we'll cover a lot of bases!"

"There are lots of people praying for Karl all over the country," Donald added. "Okay, well I'll let you know what happens." Donald and Elaine chimed in together, but not in unison, "Thanks Joni. We're praying for you, too!"

Joni felt torn. She was so looking forward to having her son with her for the holidays. She treasured his visits. What would she do for a conscience, though if Karl were out in the cold and the rain? She thought it would work out - that Karl would want to join his own family. But it wasn't happening that way. She had reservations herself as she weighed the opinions of others and words from her book on schizophrenia, "Some parents are reluctant to give autonomy to their schizophrenic children because they themselves need to continue their parental role. This is, of course, true for some parents of non-schizophrenics as well, and it often leads to retarded maturity in the young adult. It is another reason why living away from home is preferable for most released schizophrenic patients." Maybe in a way there was no going home for Karl.

"People will be coming to take care of me," Karl was giving Joni instructions again. "I'll need a lot of care when I go into Samadhi. They'll know what to do and will take care of my body."

"What are you talking about? I'm not having other people in this house. My son is coming for Christmas. You'll have to go into Samadhi some other time." *Crazy, she thought. I'm acting like this thing will happen.* Joni's face began to flush with the pink of new anger.

Karl got up and leapt out of the house as if in mortal fear of her.

Oh, boy, she thought - now what? She was bound not to go after him, but to let whatever happened happen. Sure enough, within 20 minutes he was back.

"You can't yell at me," he said in his quiet monotone. "Anyway, it's going to be okay. They said that you'll be able to take care of me here."

"I'll do what I can." Her half-hearted promise barely passed her lips in a sigh. "And I wasn't yelling - I just need to let you know that my son has to come first while he's here."

"I understand. Besides, I should be going into Samadhi tonight!"

Joni was being pulled in to his twisted reality. *What if this does happen? What if he is Jesus! - Jesus!* On the other hand she believed in the pure potential of all human beings to become enlightened, or buddhas - so was it so farfetched after all? It was one of those not infrequent times when she was thinking way too much.

The evening brought a now familiar routine. Joni made dinner. They ate and had tea from her china teapot and Karl praised the food and Joni for her efforts. Sometimes there would be conversation that bordered on the sane, but mostly there was physical silence punctuated with bursts of Karl's revelations. A song he had heard with a hidden message; the level of enlightenment of the people he came in contact with - categorized like grades of lumber; a snippet of conversation transformed into a directive from God.

And then, a sweet request to watch a movie and they would cuddle in bed. There was something different, though, about those silences. Something like heavy waves of old forgiveness. She loved him in spite of his delusions - or was it she who was deluded? At any rate, she was never much of an actress. In order to act as if she cared, she really had to care; it was that simple - and that complex.

Finally the morning came - Kevin was to arrive that evening, So much had to be accomplished at work before the holiday. "Here's a little money, in case you want to buy your folks a Christmas gift or something, "she said as she passed a twenty dollar bill to Karl in the car. "Or just get yourself some little treat, I got a little bonus - so I thought I'd share."

He took the money gingerly, in silence. Was it embarrassing for him? The air hung thick and heavy in the car.

"Thanks." His voice was quiet, but as he hopped out of the car at his drop-off point he promised to be on the seven o'clock bus, so that he could ride with Joni to the airport to greet her son. She smiled and bid him a good day once again, trying to measure his level of improvement.

Sleep had definitely improved some of his thought processes, as had the food, but was it really going anywhere? Maybe only medication could help. She had never liked that idea, but it was getting more and more feasible. Time would tell a bit more.

The seven o'clock pulled in to the parking lot on time. Joni was antsy, she had brought along a vegetarian burrito from the organic grocery store for Karl to eat on the way. There was no time to stop for dinner now - everything was clocked to the arrival of Kevin's plane. Something weird was going on. Karl was getting off the bus with some huge bags. He was beaming as he approached the car. "I did some shopping!"

Where am I going to put this? Joni was opening the trunk. The large bags were adult diapers!

"I hope that Kevin's bags fit in here, too! Why did you get diapers? What am I going to tell Kevin when he asks why I have these diapers?" It was almost funny - and almost not. There was no time to think about it, she had to get on the road. As she closed the trunk she caught a glint from something on Karl's hand. He had a channel set diamond ring on his pinkie.

"What's this?" she asked thinking he had found himself a bauble.

"This is for you," as the ring slipped off his finger and appeared in his hand in front of her face, "I want you to marry me and be my wife."

Dumbfounded, she did not resist as he placed the too big ring on her finger. She hugged him quickly and then herded him into the car. She'd have to figure something out as she drove. There was no time to waste.

"Do you like it?" he asked.

"It's beautiful, Karl, but how did you buy it?"

"I took it. They told me to when no one was looking. It's not real gold, though, I couldn't get near the real gold ones."

"Oh, it's fine," Joni's relief must have been obvious," I really don't need real jewelry, anyway - that way if it gets lost or stolen, you don't feel bad." She was fumbling for words as she fell through the rabbit hole of the situation.

"Wait 'til you see what else I got! You see, I was Santa Claus in another life, too! I just found that out today."

For the next hour, Karl pulled items out of his backpack, one by one to show Joni as she drove. Perfume, earrings, a nightshirt, candles, sweets, bath oils, atomizers, watches and a beautiful pair of brass candlesticks paraded past her like a magician's trick. It was too horrifying to cry - she had no time to go ballistic, so she opted to laugh. "You sure made $20.00 go a long way, didn't you?"

He was so happy. This was a side of him she had never seen. It was truly touching, because he had gotten gifts for her and not himself. But what would she do about this now?

The show and tell session was easier to put on than to put away. Many of the items would not fit back into the backpack, so he just stuffed them into his jacket pockets.

When they got to the terminal, however, he set off the metal detector. When asked to empty his pockets, he froze, then darted back out of the line. "I'll just wait in the car," he nervously decided.

"No, you need to stick around - just take your coat off and run it through the conveyor belt." She was not about to let him take her car keys, and/or wander off to parts unknown in the International airport.

"I'll just wait in the car," his voice was begging now - "I've got all that stuff in my pockets and it still has the price tags on it..."

"C'mon, Karl, just take off your jacket and we'll put it through. You didn't take any guns or anything, did you?" The thought hadn't occurred to her until just then.

"No. Okay." He took off his coat and it went through the x-ray conveyor as he passed through the arch successfully.

"I know that your heart was sincere and I deeply appreciate the gifts," she started, trying carefully to think before each word, "but, you know that stealing is wrong and this can't happen again. It's a bad cause for you, honey."

He nodded in agreement, but said nothing. Staring straight ahead, his eyes downcast as if a severely scolded child he acquiesced to his better judgment. He was shaking, so they stopped to have a drink, now that the time was finally on their side again. The plane wasn't due for another 40 minutes.

Karl was calming down now as he sat and stared at people in the crowded bar. Joni had a diet Coke while he sipped his cappuccino. "Can I sit here?" The voice came through the din and seemed to be emanating from a burly, beaming, weathered face of a man with a mug of beer.

"Sure," piped Joni. Karl nodded with what was enthusiasm for him. *I hope he doesn't tell this guy he's Jesus, she thought.* "Where are you headed?" she ventured.

"I'm on my way home for the holidays," was the wistful reply. "I've been at sea for about eight months now - over near Russia. My family is in Illinois." He was friendly, but with an air of sadness. He definitely looked the part to Joni and she was pleased that Karl seemed to be at least nodding amiably, even somewhat engaged in the conversation.

"I'd better check the gate," she said as she excused herself to step just outside the bar and look for signs of the flight's arrival.

"Mom! Where have you been?" Kevin was alone with the flight attendant. He was now 16 years old and a good 11 inches taller than his mom. His blonde hair barely visible under his SF Giants baseball cap, his deep blue eyes flashed at her.

"Hi, sweetie! How come you're here already? Were you the first one off the plane?" "No, I was the last one off and I've been waiting here for about 15 minutes!"

"Well, the plane was early then - you're still not due to be here for another 10 minutes! Sorry, honey - let's go. You need to meet Karl - he's the guy I told you about who will be staying with us."

"Where is he?"

"In the bar, let's go."

After the introductions, Kevin opted to go down to the baggage claim area rather than wait for Karl to finish his coffee. Joni was torn, but felt it was for the best, since Karl was not going to be able to talk normally with Kevin. In minutes they joined Kevin at the carousel and mother and son began to catch up on the latest family news.

Karl tried to come out of his shell and talk a bit. He genuinely seemed to like Kevin and on the way home, as Joni drove; Kevin fell asleep in the back seat.

"Don't worry about his face," said Karl softly, "I had that problem when I was his age, too. It's a very hurtful thing, but it's good, because it makes you humble." He was referring to the acne that had bloomed since Joni had last seen her son. Karl's concern and compassion touched her deeply. She, too, had known the agony of teenaged acne, but wondered if she would ever have had the courage to say to a parent what he just had.

Once home, Kevin was tucked in and Karl settled onto his cot, which now occupied the living room. "Tonight should be the night!" he said to Joni. "I should be in Samadhi by the morning!"

"Well, it may not happen for many years, yet, Karl. Don't worry if it isn't tonight." She had seen him become euphoric at the thought of his eminent Samadhi only to be crushed and humiliated when in the morning he awoke a mere mortal after all. His thinking was clearly not moving very quickly toward health, but neither did it seem to be regressing. All she hoped at this point was that she and her son would enjoy a happy Christmas vacation, with the added enjoyment of a pleasant visit with Karl.

The next day it seemed she'd get her wish. As she did gongyo, Karl and Kevin set up his new stereo and played some comedy tapes. Karl was enthralled and laughed wildly with Kevin - a sight heretofore inconceivable to Joni. This might be medicine for him after all, she thought.

As usual, Kevin could be counted on to be gracious and compassionate. Joni couldn't have been prouder of her son.

Later, as they shopped, she turned to Kevin and as she often did, asked for his opinion. "Do I just give Karl the shirt that I bought or do I go out on a limb, spend money I don't really have, and get him a cowboy hat?"

"Get him a hat, Mom! I'll help you pick one out. It's Christmas and he won't be getting many presents to open." There was no hesitation in his voice. Once again, Joni felt deep pride and connection with her generous and genuine son.

"I wish there was a grown man just like you..." she said implying the obvious. "Well in a couple of years there will be!" he quipped back in a flash.

"Yeah, but you're my son..." she laughed.

Christmas morning came quickly and both Kevin and Joni were anxious to see Karl's face when they presented him with the gift they had saved for last. As he opened it up, his face lit up and he gently placed the hat on his head.

"It's just the color I would have chosen myself! And it fits just fine! Thank you."

"Kevin picked it out, "said Joni, "we hope you'll enjoy wearing it dancing!"

"It looks really good on you!" Kevin piped in. "You guys should go dancing tonight!" "Not tonight, Kev'."

"Why not?"

"It's Christmas, that's why - nothing's open!"

"Oh, yeah - well then tomorrow you guys should go dancing."

"We'll see," Joni was sounding parental again.

"Let's go for a walk," said Karl as he gently took Joni's hand.

"Okay! Sure!" She was ready to go in the blink of an eye. As they walked, Karl talked and talked about his days with Easwaran and how hard he had worked. He recounted the story of being thrown off the ashram for working too hard. He had wanted to work all night - his labor was donated - but they had told him not to work all night. So when he did anyway, they had bodily removed him from the premises.

"Can you believe it? Here this man is talking about non-violence and he doesn't even realize that I did a totally non-violent act against him! He was supposed to help me to prepare for my Samadhi! Of all of the people who should know who I am, he should!"

"You should write about this," Joni encouraged him. "Your experiences are truly valuable - perhaps that's the whole reason you had to go through them - so that you could write about them and help others to avoid the pitfalls you've seen." She was hoping her words were being received, but it was hard to tell, because a long silence fell as she stopped speaking.

They walked along the side of the road on their way back now. He adjusted his stride to match hers, for which she was grateful. A scant five feet tall, she found walking with most people meant a jog for her even as they strolled comfortably.

"Well, you know, I don't write," Karl was blurting out his reasoning after an agonizingly long thought process. "You know Socrates said you should never write. He didn't write anything down, you know."

"Well, that may be - but someone, somewhere wrote what he had to say, otherwise, how would you know he ever said that?" Inside Joni cursed her lack of knowledge. She wanted specifics. She wanted to be able to counter Karl's reasoning with educated and intelligent debate so that he could be led back to reason. She had hit a chord.

"That's right, "murmured Karl as they skinnied up on the shoulder to let a car go by.

He seemed to have been hit by a ton of mental bricks. She could see the wheels turning in his head. "But, I still don't think I can write," he said.

"Well, you might try taping; dictating. If you couldn't write a book you might be able to talk a book!" She wasn't going to give up until the final mental tumbler fell into locked position - when it did; she knew that all conversation would abruptly end. She understood that this was due to overload and that he needed time to regroup mentally.

"Talk a book... Taco Bell," he laughed, enjoying his own puns and twists of words.

Then, the tumbler locked in and they finished the walk home in silence.

The weather had turned brisk - or at least what now passed for brisk, since Joni had become acclimated to Northern California. She laughed to herself at how she once went all winter with just a sweater - when she was newly from the East. Karl, too had been a Californian now for ten years. He felt the cold now at 50 degrees and wondered how he ever survived the Minnesota winters of minus tens and fifteens. His vague memories of hunting at the lake and pole vaulting at high school drifted by his inner eye as if he was looking at snapshots of another man's life. He reached for Joni's hand and walked along in without a word, they both felt happy and connected - even though they were worlds apart.

"I want a picture of us," he said, "wearing our cowboy hats!"

"I think Barbara could do that for us," Joni replied. Barbara was a fellow Buddhist and she had gone along with the "mission" of rescuing Karl in support of Joni all the way. They went to see her later in the same week and had the

104

photos developed soon after that. The pictures were fun. They showed Karl clearly happy sharp looking in his new cowboy hat over his shaven head. Joni was smiling, too, but to those who knew her, there was an element of a lie in her smile. She placed them on the stone mantel in the living room. She wanted to send copies to his parents, but hadn't gotten around to making more just yet. There was time, she thought.

Several days later, Karl came to her.

"I've written out all you'll need to tell the paramedics when they come," Karl was referring again to his Samadhi. "I'll need a binder for this and do you have any stencils? I want to make the first page look really good."

"I've got just what you need." She darted off to a cabinet where she kept her 'art' supplies. Bringing forth some rub-on letters and a shiny new red binder, she presented them to him.

He was tickled to the bone as he set about the task of making his title page. He would not show it to her, though, until it was done the next morning.

When she read it she retained her poker-faced cool, but inside she was screaming - somebody help this guy! She hoped that Kevin's pre-occupation with his friends would keep him from seeing this or worse, asking questions about it.

It read in bold type on the title page, "THIS IS THE LORD. PLEASE USE EXTREME CARE!! NOT A COMA - OVER IN 7-10 DAYS. DO NOT SHOCK. NO DRUGS - Except Mild Stimulants."

The pages that followed had been printed out on the computer at the college. They were informative and at the same time tangible proof of his need for psychological help. They were so well written that under other circumstances they might be taken as scholarly. Joni read each page carefully:

TO THE DOCTORS/PARAMEDICS IN CHARGE OF ME:

"You've found yourselves a mountain of dynamite. My age is 31. For 12 years, beginning at age 18, I practiced intense spiritual disciplines under a guru, Eknath Easwaran, who has since proven to be false. Toward the end of this period, when I was 26, God, the Creator, began communicating with me in exactly the same way as he spoke to Abraham, Moses, David and Jesus.

God told me that I was "in front," and that my function was to serve his voice. I have always done this. We are all going through a process of reincarnation, being born anew every 100 years or so. I was born as the men listed above as well as Rama, Krishna, the Buddha, Mohammed, Nanak (Sikhism), Zoroaster, Lao-tse, Socrates, Mahavir (Jainism), Chaitanya, Ramakrishna and others.

Let me point out that the words "Lord" and "God" are not interchangeable. By "God" I mean the Creator, who does not have a body. YHWH is his true name. He is the King. The word "Lord" signifies his messenger or spokesman. It is because God has always wanted to communicate with men that he takes someone into Samadhi. This is being called the Lord. Here is the dynamite: all the world's scriptures come from me. Every religion was started by the same person, in different births….

I've been instructed to tell you this immediately because of my mission to unite all religions through the medium of television."

Joni put down the manifesto to take a breath. For someone who didn't want to write there were pages and pages of explanation according to Karl.

"Before, disciples were necessary to ask good questions and disseminate my teachings. Now I can go directly to the world, giving talks to each religion in turn, explaining what has happened and what I mean to them now. ...

Jesus said, "The powers of space will be bent" and "the Son of Man will come on a cloud in great glory to gather people from the four corners of the earth." For someone who didn't even know about electricity, this is a startling accurate description of television.

Now Jesus said he would send a "witness". That's me. For years I've had divine power—the power to observe God and communicate with him through the unconscious minds of those around me. You see, although I haven't been perfected, my consciousness is already the deepest on the planet. For this reason I see everything and everyone rising out of God, but imagine my predicament! I did not have the power to speak or make anyone believe me. No money, no friends, yet the heaviest responsibility imaginable.

Most of my twenties were spent meditating 2-4 hours every day and holding a regular job or going to school. This last year a regular job would have interfered seriously in God's plans, so I was forced to eat in soup kitchens and steal small items necessary for life. This is why Jesus said he would come like a "thief in the night", unrecognized by society and not supported.

There was a person God arranged to help me—it was the woman who was Mary Magdalene in Jesus' day. She had a spiritual experience which enabled her to recognize me. She chose not to help me and forfeited her experience in the next life, which will be given to a man instead, whose identity I know. It made things rough for me, and really the whole world lost because of her." (Joni knew he was referring to his former girlfriend Corrine. How hard it is to be in love, she thought),

No soul ever gets lost or goes backwards. YWHW is pushing the whole thing forward, but it is a real world and there is only room for a few at the top. He is fighting to maintain and advance life against heavy odds. Although he is very powerful, very mighty, we need to learn to be a little sympathetic and cooperative. Remember that without him there would be just empty space.

Now come the women. I believe the sudden explosion of shelled fossils which no one understands was due to the speed added to evolution after the introduction of females and the increased genetic mix. God explained to me that the effect was not immediate, but very dramatic.

The consciousness of women is very interesting. This is going to shock the world, but in truth they do not think for themselves. They arose to help us and in fact "pick up" words which "float" around us and are beneficial to us. It's the best

108

way I can describe what they do. Their consciousness is in some way derived from men.

They are not very good at this however. Their speech gets to be really offensive after a while. Although they do not really care, they say they do, which makes it really difficult to see the truth which Jesus said would set us free. When men have evolved far enough to see this we will have something like Plato's Republic, where the men hold the women and children in common. However, God has told me that we will develop the genetic technology to reproduce men without the need for women. He explained that souls will have no trouble in genetically engineered bodies."

Holy Cow! Thought Joni – this is ridiculous. He's got issues beyond schizophrenia.

She hated herself for doing it, but she read on.

"God has been watching us throughout the long period of evolution and he is by no means done with the human race. He plans for us to be here longer than the dinosaurs, perhaps even billions of years, except that we will be evolving into higher and higher species. The next species will be all male and it will have some ability which is higher than thinking. (This won't be for thousands of years, unless we speed things up using genetic technology, which is probable).

Oh yes! God knew that we would split the atom, but he also made sure we would be civilized enough not to blow ourselves up. Here is how: imagine the world without all of the people I've listed. Wouldn't it still be the stone ages? So he has told *us enough to speed our development and still assure we wouldn't destroy ourselves. Pollution also will be overcome.*

Life does have meaning and what we do does matter. This is going to blow your mind. When our sun dies and life is killed on this planet, our souls are kept and will be transferred to a new, young sun. (This has happened in the past). There the whole process of evolution will take place again except that it will be faster, and we will be much better.

Everyone has a dim awareness of this. When you think of heaven this is what you mean. Our relationships, for instance, will be much smoother. Many more people will follow the Ten Commandments, which, if you think about a world without killing, stealing, adultery and covetousness, really would be heaven on earth. You see, God gave us the key to everything right away.

As near as I can tell, this process will continue forever. I'm fairly certain the universe goes through cyclic big bangs, but YHWH has shown me that every little act of ours will still be felt in each new universe. You can be sure that if you are good you will thank yourself later, and this process will never end. Do you see how hopeful my message is starting to look? ...

God has told me that because of the accumulation of lives I'm spiritually many times the size of Jesus. I beg you to take this seriously. This is really the beginning of a new epoch, by far the most important moment in history. Using television I will be able to unite all the world's religions and secure a peace which will last, and I can assure everyone I will be back in 100 years. Many rapid changes will take place, resulting in what Jesus called "the kingdom without end."

However, the quality of my experience matters. If you follow the directions I gave you I can go higher and will return better able to do this job. Promoting circulation, feeding through intubation, dilute oxygen and mild stimulants will all help, as would 24 hour care. Please be careful; the future of mankind is in your hands. This is going to happen to me more than once, but by that time I will be well known and this won't be much of a problem. Convince yourself of the truth of my claims and then act on it.

Signed: J. Karl Jackson"

Joni was awash with mixed emotions. Disgust at the belief system which had led him to this - was he brainwashed at the ashram? She felt anger at his low opinion of women - especially since she was the one who most tried to help him. She felt curious and amazed at the intertwining of his thoughts and philosophies…a decided Christian, but very much involved with the scientific idea of evolution; preaching the Ten Commandments, but admittedly stealing, himself. The concept of reincarnation overlaid on prevalent 'End Times' time frames and this Hindu Samadhi as the centerpiece of it all. She was determined to learn more and would read up on Ramakrishna with any spare moments she could muster from her already overloaded days. Threads of truth were woven throughout the piece - and that was hopeful. How could a brain so filled with knowledge be so far from health? The dichotomy of her own thoughts was menacing. Maybe a copy of his work to the right person could open up doors. This was physical proof of his mental state.

Oppression

Nature in darkness groans
And men are bound to sullen contemplation in the night:
Restless they turn on beds of sorrow; in their inmost brain
Feeling the crushing wheels, they rise, they write the bitter
words
Of stern philosophy & knead the bread of knowledge with tears
& groans.

- William Blake

Chapter Six   Illusion

Joni had begun to believe the illusion that Karl was returning to normal and now that illusion was shattered. But her mind held that in his lucid moments, his keen wit and intelligence just couldn't be sickness. Or if he <u>was</u> sick - which variety was it? He was moody enough to be manic depressive, or bi-polar, but the psychiatrist had said he was schizophrenic. What was the difference? It seemed like there really wasn't enough of a difference to be sure. Could he have both diseases? Then, too, the books cautioned about religious experiences and said how ecstatic religious experience is by all appearances the same in terms of symptomology as schizophrenia. The bad part, it seemed to Joni, was that many a schizophrenic believed he or she *was* a religious figure such as Christ - but the documented states of bliss for saints and gurus were accepted as real - as weird as they may have seemed. Joan of Arc had heard voices; St John Bosco was at one point thought to be insane. Her head flew in a million directions and re-grouped time and again. What was going on? Why did this gentle man seem so excruciatingly sensitive? Why would he not listen to reason at some times and be perfectly logical to the point of deep philosophy at others? One thing seemed certain to Joni - this man needed expression of something boiling inside, something reaching a quantum measure beyond containment.

One evening during Kevin's visit, he and Joni got to the mall to pick Karl up, but they were almost an hour early. As she drove by hoping against hope that Karl would be early, too - they were chagrined to find no one waiting for them. They were thinking the same way, as they often did; there wasn't really any time or need to go shopping, yet it was going to be a long wait. Joni rarely had moments like this - not already spoken for, that is. They could just wait in the car and spend a few minutes resting. She could take a fifteen minute nap and be totally refreshed at almost any time of the day. Kevin was squirming, but sympathetic to her exhaustion. She found a place to park and gently put the back of her seat down to rest. "Are we just going to sit here?" He asked in disbelief.

"Yes, just let me take a quick nap, maybe he'll get out a little early - but it won't be that long now."

"Maaaaaa," he whined, "C'mon…can't we come back?"

"Honey, we could, but there's no sense in driving around. We can't go all the way home…and besides, I just need a little rest." Joni was gentle, but firm. She had no intention of trying to think of a more entertaining plan at this point. She closed her eyes as she spoke, hoping her son would have mercy on her. For a few minutes there was silence. She relaxed a little, then felt the car rustle a little under her.

"Here comes the security truck..." Kevin was trying to make conversation. Joni was noting the flashing yellow lights through slitted eyes as she rested.

"He's just making the rounds," she said.

"I know!" Kevin became animated, "Let's play dead! Then when the security guy drives by he'll see two dead bodies in the car! Don't move! Here he comes!" With that Kevin threw his seat back and assumed a dead guy position with eyes opened and staring and a slight dribble of drool coming from the corner of his mouth.

Joni took one look at him and began to laugh. This kid is such a character, she thought. She appreciated him - perhaps more than he would ever realize.

"Act dead!" Kevin ordered - "He's coming back!"

"Okay," Joni laughed as she closed her eyes and stilled herself. His enthusiasm had carried the call and she was caught up in the silly game.

"Okay, he's gone..." Kevin was relenting now. The routine of assuming the position repeated several times in between "What time is it?" checks. Mother and son laughed at themselves and there was so much more unsaid. They both agreed that Kevin would have news for his friends when he got back to New York. "Yeah, I'll just tell them...oh, what did I do in California? I played dead in the parking lot with my mom! - They should really be impressed with that one!"

"Well, you just can't beat the kind of classy entertainment I provide," Joni was sure this could start a major migration of his friends wanting to experience her talent for fun! The time passed, Karl appeared at the appointed moment and they all went home together.

115

"Have Fun!" Kevin chimed as his mother and her friend went off to go dancing. Karl would wear his new hat - it was an exciting time in a way. Joni's optimism at seeing him 'fit in' a bit more was well rewarded as one after one the regular dancers commented to Karl on how much they liked his hat. He was in his glory, but also cautious to keep his cool. He danced mainly with other people, saving Joni for what she called charity dances (when no one else was available), but she didn't mind. She was sure she was seeing a normal man emerge from the rubble - at least a man who would have the desire to work toward a more normal life for sure. But life was seldom as easy as the vision Joni held.

Joni had to work, even though the holidays were usually a slow time at the office. She felt it was best for Karl to continue his routine of going into town each day as well. The last thing she wanted was for him to get comfortable just staying at her home each day, watching TV or doing even less. So, as usual, she dropped him off and he promised to take the 7 o'clock bus home.

At six o'clock the phone rang. "Is this Joni Mathews?"

"Yes, it is," Joni was in a good mood just preparing dinner. She and her son were enjoying some lighthearted banter.

"This is Thrifty's drug store - John Jackson wanted us to call you and tell you that he won't be on the 7 o'clock bus. He's being detained."

"Is he all right? What happened?"

"He's being detained for shoplifting and the police are taking him into custody.

That's all I can tell you."

"What do I do? Do I need to like bail him out or something?" She was canceling the thought even as it came out of her mouth. No way could she afford to bail anybody out of anywhere, nor did she really want to. He had promised not to take any more stuff.

"Why don't you try calling the police department in about an hour or so? They'll have more information for you then."

She thought to herself - maybe, if I feel like it..."Okay, thanks," she answered.

"What was that about?" asked Kevin.

"Well, it seems Karl was shoplifting and has been arrested." She was never much at beating around the bush.

"Is he in jail?"

"I guess so, but don't worry about it. I'll find out the details later. Actually, as long as he's safe, it's okay. I may have to go and get him or something, but I don't know yet."

Kevin wanted to know what he had stolen - so did Joni, but neither one was prepared for the answer when Joni finally talked to the police.

"He was stealing adult diapers and Ensure", the officer ventured slowly. "Do you have any idea why he would be taking such items?"

Joni was enraged, "Yes, I know why - because he's nuts and he thinks he's going into this state of Samadhi and will be incontinent during that time! - It's kind of a long story. He really needs help."

"Is he your boyfriend?"

"No, I've just been letting him stay here to keep him off the street. His parents want him back in Minneapolis, but he won't go. They want him to get help."

"Well, okay. We're going to keep him in jail for a few days. It sounds as if it might be a good thing to at least keep him taken care of for a while. Maybe this will convince him to get help."

"I sure hope so. What do I do next?"

"Well, the court will need to put his case on the calendar, and after that it's up to him what happens next. In all probability he will be allowed out and appointed an attorney, then we'll go from there."

"So I should call the court?"

"Yes give them this case number 93zx56821, and they'll let you know when he'll be out. It will probably be 2 or 3 days."

"Okay."

Joni hung up the phone, her face ashen. Kevin stood by trying to figure out the other half of the conversation he had overheard.

"What was he stealing, Mom?" "Depends."

"Depends on what?"

"No, Depends – Adult diapers."

"Diapers! Why in the world would he be taking diapers?" Kevin was laughing and disgusted at the same time.

"Well, honey, I didn't want to tell you this, but Karl thinks he's going into some religious state called Samadhi…"

"And he's going to shit himself?"

Joni couldn't help laughing, too. "Yeah," she gasped between giggles "and he wanted *me* to take care of him - because he thinks this is the way to enlightenment!"

"Right, Mom, you have to shit your pants to become enlightened. Su-u-u-u-ure." He rolled his eyes delighted that he had made his mother lose control with laughter once again.

"What happens if you puke at the same time? Do you go straight to heaven or something?"

"Okay, okay, I know," Joni was regaining control. "I know it sounds weird, but in India, this is a real thing that has happened - and we have to respect other people's religions, so let's try not to make fun of Karl's beliefs."

"Hey, in case you haven't noticed - we're not in India - and Mom, no one goes into Samdali or whatever you call it here!"

"Well, I know, and the fact of the matter is, Karl needs help. But, he does base his beliefs on things that he has read about and studied, it's just that he's also schizophrenic, I think."

"Great, Mom! Just great! Here you try to help this guy out by giving him a place to stay and taking him in for Christmas and all and he goes out and steals diapers! I don't hate the guy, and I wouldn't want him to be sleeping on the street, but why don't his parents get him?"

"They've tried, but he won't go home." "Well he can't stay here forever, either!"

"Of course not. I never expected him to be here this long. But once it was Christmas and all, I just couldn't throw him out...." Joni was feeling torn again. Was it selfish for her to have forced her son to share his holiday vacation with this lunatic? Would it have been a better lesson for her to have taught her son self-preservation above compassion? Was this compassion or just weirdness on her part? She remembered the previous Christmastime Kevin had spent with her. It had been two years ago already. They had gone into town on Christmas Eve and had seen a man on the side of the road with a sign that read 'Will Work For Food'. Kevin had been so upset. He wanted to take him home for Christmas. He couldn't bear the thought of the poor guy going hungry.

"Can't we bring him home for dinner at least, Mom? What's he going to do on Christmas? No one will be working on Christmas. We have enough, don't we?"

"Kevin, we can't just bring home strangers off the street," Joni had replied, "besides, some of these people are really doing okay - some of them aren't really homeless at all..."

"Please, Mom, please," he had begged. "He doesn't look like he's faking - at least we could give him a few bucks."

"Well, I'll tell you what...if he's still there on our way back, we can stop and at least talk to him, okay?" But when they returned, the man had vanished...and Joni was thankful...and Kevin seemed sad, but somewhat relieved...and that was that.

She didn't bring it up now, directly, but she could see that the wheels were turning in his head, too and that he was remembering that Christmas past. It's funny how history can repeat itself.

"Well, Karl won't be out until after you've gone," confirmed Joni as she hung up the phone.

"Good!" quipped Kevin. He had had enough intrigue for one trip and was enjoying his time with and 'undivided' Mom.

"I'm glad, too," said Joni, "Because we needed to have some time together. I'm hoping this will lead to real help for Karl. I'm going to visit him tomorrow and see if the experience has cleared up his mental processes at all - - - and to let him know he's got a friend. He must feel so alone. You know, I think that what happened to you with Ed may have happened to Karl, too. There may be some way that you can help him."

Kevin was not biting. He did not want to think about it. It was a thought that never needed confirmation or commitment; just a thought floating on the feather of a wish. A wish to somehow right the wrongs of the past - as if they could ever be.

He didn't want to be reminded of the abuse by his stepdad, Ed. He didn't want to be reminded that he had kept it a secret until Ed was long gone from Joni's life. He didn't want to think about the fact that despite keeping his secret, his father had taken him back to New York when he was only 8. The scene at the police station when his mother came to say goodbye, her helplessness, even with her written statement that he had wanted to live with her. None of it had made sense then, it still didn't. But the pain of that moment, for all of his trying to protect his mother, was still unbearable eight years later. He was almost old enough now to demand to come back to her and his father would not legally be able to stop him.

The jail was not a friendly place, but it seemed less ominous than Joni had expected. New red brick-like blocks

121

made up the outside and the high ceilings inside the lobby gave it an almost ritzy feel. It took four tries for Joni to get through the metal detectors. Earrings, bracelet, rings watch and finally hair clips had to be removed. Just when she thought they would need to have her fillings removed from her teeth, she passed through without the telltale buzzers and lights flashing. Inside the thick cubicle, she waited on white plastic stacking chairs. She was glad that there were two - since she was too short to see through the thick Plexiglas window on just one. There were no phone-like things to use, just some holes drilled through the plastic glass to the other side. It was the echo of the chamber itself that propelled the sound through the thickness so that communication was possible, albeit with effort.

Karl looked thinner in his V-necked navy chemise and matching pull on pants. This outfit was reminiscent of interns' scrubs, not like the street style clothes that the tough guys wear in the made-for-TV movies. Humiliation was in order.

"I'm really in jail," he said still trying to wake from a disconnected dream. "I thought about telling them who I am. Last night I thought maybe it was going to happen in here - that would have been interesting. I can just see the look on their faces when they realize what a big mistake they've made…"

"Are you doing okay?" Joni was hoping to keep him on the reality trail. "What is going to happen? Do you know how long you'll be in here?" She stopped, almost forgetting how confused he would get when more than one question was fired at him.

"It should be a few days. I have to go to court. They gave me a lawyer. She said I was lucky, because the things I took were less than $50. If they had been more than that I would have had a felony."

122

"You are lucky, Karl. Your parents are worried about you, too."

"I told you not to talk to them. Did they call you? How did they get your number?" He was clearly agitated.

"The police told them," Joni lied. She hadn't let on that she was having fairly regular chats with his parents because he had been dead set against communicating with them. "They want to do what they can to help." This was the truth. Karl's father had pulled every string he knew. He had gotten influential people to write letters to the judge on Karl's behalf. He had written requesting that Karl receive help. He was desperate to get help for his son, short of mortgaging his family's entire future. There was no law that would allow for Karl's deportation to his parents' home. He was 31 years old and in some ways capable of caring for himself. More than anything else the catchall roadblock was ever in place; he was not a danger to himself or others according to the law. Obvious to all who knew him, he *was* a danger to himself - but the law wanted to see something more along the lines of suicide. More a case of damned if you don't - because if you do and are successful, society has no more problem with you - case closed. Joni shivered at the thought - *maybe that's the plan.*
Surely, this situation had no easy answers - but what frustrated her was that there were no answers at all. She was flying by the seat of her pants, wrapped up in something she felt morally compelled to do, yet there was no logical reason for why she even cared. She hoped along with his parents, that the judge would order psychiatric help for Karl and that in a short season he would be back to normal. This was the only logical route that she could see.

Jail time would do him no good. A fine might propel him back into work - but it was iffy at best as to whether or not he *could* work given his current state of mind. It had been impossible to meaningfully look for work without an address or phone at which an employer could contact him. And, he was bound and determined not to stay at the shelters - he was bulldog stubborn on that one. Time alone would tell what the final answer would be.

"You'll probably need to get a job when you get out - to pay your fine and all," Joni was more suggesting than telling him. "Do you think you will?"

"Maybe", said Karl slowly. "I'll think about it. It all depends on what God wants me to do."

He was looking down again. He looked to be in a trance-like state during these times. His thin arms crossed at the waist and wrapping loosely around his frame as he sat bent forward slightly. "Well, thanks for coming, "Karl said shyly, "it made me feel good. Bye - I'll call you when I get out."

"Okay, honey, bye...take care," Joni's eyes felt hot as she watched him turn on his heels and go back out to the cells which she would never see. What a strange world seemed to exist beyond the thick, stuffy cubicles. But, she did not cry. This man has survived the streets for over a year, she thought, a place like this is probably a piece of cake for him. Thank goodness it's little Santa Rosa California and not Chicago or somewhere even more scary.

"We've faxed letters to the judge and I've got my friend, who's a District Attorney out here to contact the District Attorney out there. That could help. The judge *has* to order help for Karl, then we'll be home free. Once he gets help, we'll be able to get him home again." Donald was excited as Joni listened filled with hope.

"I think we're in the home stretch," she chimed in.

"Oh, Joni, we're so thankful for your help! God bless you!"

Elaine was on the extension. She had been keeping body and soul together with her work and prayer groups. She taught developmentally disabled children. Ironic in a way. Her Bible study group had put Karl on their prayer lists for years. They were certainly thrilled to know the progress that had been made in recent weeks. Everyone felt that the arrest had been a blessed intervention.

Donald was back in control of the conversation now, "You know, Karl will thank you for this someday."

"Yes! He will!" agreed Elaine.

"Well, whether he does or not," said Joni, "I'm doing what I feel I have to do. I am worried for his life - so I don't really care if he hates my guts, as long as he stays *alive*. I'll keep you posted on what happens in court."

"Okay - thanks a lot! We'll talk to you soon!"

Finally, thought Joni, this thing is really going to come to a conclusion. I sure hope that Karl sees how much his parents care and that he'll accept that he needs to go back to them until he can get on his feet again.

That night as she did gongyo in front of her altar she cried. All the mind pictures that had haunted her seemed to be dissipating. No more tearful flights to Minneapolis alongside his dead body. No more 'we did the best we could' graveside excuses. She strengthened in her conscious thought the picture of Karl lecturing at the University level. This was the alternative she had always seen, but couldn't always keep afloat in her mind. Yes! He was going to be okay - and he would still have enough life left to make up for lost time! He was going to be able to contribute what he was *really* meant to do in this life and it would not be insignificant! She was filled with appreciation and hope. It was still unclear as to how he would get through the imminent counseling or as to whether medication would be needed. More likely than not, it would be, at least temporarily. That part would be hard, but if Karl had moral support, it should work out okay. His attorney, Stephanie Joy, would have him evaluated again by Dr. Apostle. The irony of the names in this case made Joni smile to herself. How can 'J.C.' as she had jokingly called him, not think he's Jesus when he has to go and see his 'Apostle' as ordered by 'Joy'?

It seemed as though Karl was deciding to face the music and agree to some kind of treatment. He had a little over a month before his case came up on the court calendar. He had a $75.00 fine to pay. His writing had become an obsession. He wrote limericks, poetry and was working on re-writing the dictionary. Despite this, there were moments of triumph.

On January 14th, Joni's letter to Donald and Elaine read:

Dear Donald and Elaine,

Yesterday was our best ever! On the way home Karl pointed out where his psychiatrist is. He said he could walk from the mall, but I told him I'd take him and be with him through this.

Then - after dinner we watched a movie - he talked more than ever like a normal person - but the best part was after the movie we got joking around and he had me <u>in stitches for two hours!</u> He had eaten too much for dinner so was doing "slug" imitations - then we moved to pigs and I said he could go into pig Samadhi - we both laughed and carried on - it was just wonderful! He did go to his Samadhi bed, but in the morning when he came back we started joking again - he's laughing openly - we both have the punster type of humor-

I'm more hopeful than ever that he is _healing_! Our miracle is happening - believe it!

Love, Joni

She savored the scenes from the night before. She had served buckwheat noodles and Karl had raved about them. He enjoyed them so much, that he ate beyond capacity to the point near melt-down, but it brought out a joyous side of him. "Are you sure you don't want any dessert?" she asked smiling. Karl had rolled around on the floor playfully. "I couldn't' even eat the tip of a chocolate chip!" He laughed at the thought as did Joni. By now they were both envisioning a very large balloon like roly- poly guy biting off the tip of a chocolate chip and exploding into a million pieces. They were in uncontrollable fits of laughter. To make it even more hilarious, Karl began talking with a Southern accent and walking like a cowboy. Just the contrast of the sight made Joni double over, gasping for air as she laughed. This was a time she would not soon forget. Karl had decided it was quite memorable as well and resolved to write a comedy play called, "The Tip Of A Chocolate Chip." Joni agreed he could have a best seller - this was the kind of thing she wanted to encourage. Her reverence for laughter had been borne out by one of her writing heroes, Norman Cousins. It wasn't just a jolly time, it was a healing.

Karl had been going nightly to his cot still set up in the living room in order to go into Samadhi, but Joni knew there were other clouds afoot. He was still a virgin according to his writings, and she had certainly not changed that. She could feel his conflict around the subject. It was a painful place to be. His humor and wit had thrown her into a whole new level of enjoyment of him. He was capable of so much - and few people had ever made her laugh the way he did. A tragic and sweet realization swept through her heart.

The miracle of health soon vanished with the reality of illness. He had merely been in his manic phase - and now the equal but opposite depression was again overtaking his soul. Joni read what he had written as he stayed up all night:

"Happiness is a stupid state of mind. If you feel that you are happy you are in trouble. Make tracks. Throw it away. If you live with illusions I will not talk to you. You will never see me. Don't do what you want to do. See yourself destroyed when it is all taken away. Love - never had any, never wanted any."

Court day came on January 18th. Joni took time off from work to meet Karl at the courthouse and just be present with him as he went before the judge. She had no idea what would happen next. Stephanie Joy was there and stood with Karl when his case was called. The charges were read, petty theft. When the judge asked what was stolen and the D.A. had to reply "adult diapers", two young men in the front row snickered to each other in what would otherwise have been howling laughter. Joni was embarrassed for Karl and at the same time hoping he wouldn't do anything even more embarrassing. The Judge mentioned that he had gotten letters from Karl's parents and that they had wanted him to get treatment. He asked for the recommendation from Karl's attorney.

She asked for an extensive evaluation and treatment if required, but when the judge asked who would pay for it, she had no good answer. The judge and D.A. were decidedly against the idea of using taxpayers' money for such a purpose and the judge ultimately ruled that they would not. He admonished Karl to get himself help or get a job. Then the payoff came: "I understand that a Joni Mathews is letting you stay at her place?"

"Yes," said Karl.

"Well, maybe she can help you," the judge continued, "at any rate I hereby order that you stay with her - understand? You are not to leave her place, unless she throws you out or you'll be in violation of your probation."

Joni felt a kind of this-isn't-really-happening stunned. Can he *do* that? So - no evaluation and Karl is ordered to stay with me! Wow! What in the world will I get myself into next?

Outside the courtroom Karl turned to Joni and smiled, "I want you to pay my fine, "he said as though it was her grand privilege to do so.

"No, I won't," said Joni flatly. She didn't know if his father would send the money to the court or not, but she wasn't going to pay a fine after clearly admonishing him not to steal.

"Why not?" he demanded, "It's only $75.00 - you would have bought me a jacket..." "Karl, I don't have the money for one thing..."

"You must have some money tucked away somewhere," he insisted.

"Karl, do you understand what bankruptcy is? I'm that close, and beside which, I didn't steal anything!"

Karl ran away like a spoiled child.

"Karl!" Joni ran after him. "Come on. Let's go for a ride."

"No! I want to walk!" he snapped.

"Okay, then can I walk with you?"

He softened and began to walk. She followed by his side in silence. She knew that conversation was out for the moment.

"I wrote a poem for you today," he said sweetly. "Only I don't have it with me right now. But I can write another one…" he began writing on the small notebook that he carried in his shirt pocket.

He handed her the verse:

To Joni

Oh sweetheart! The clouds and violets open for you, as does the Milky Way.
The stars shine for you. The lake has waves for you.
The hummingbird flies for you. What more could you ask for?

"How do you like it?" he asked eagerly.

Joni felt that lying was in order at this point. It clearly meant nothing to him and was some sort of ploy, but she was not about to trample on his feelings - just in case. "It's very nice," she said without flourish.

"Do you think it's worth $75.00?" he asked.

"No!" Joni snapped back. "You gave this to me as a gift! I'm not paying for it - and I'm not paying your fine!" She expected Karl to run away again and she was perfectly ready to let him run. He sensed it, naturally, and didn't budge. After 5 minutes of silence or so, Joni suggested that they drive to the beach to clear their heads. Karl agreed, but was obviously depressed.

The ocean air and sounds seemed to help. All was in perspective once again beside the endless sight of ocean waves and coastline. Karl ran and then came back and put his

130

arm around Joni's shoulders. "It's going to be all right," she said. There was a battle going on in Karl, between the acceptance of fact and the belief he had fashioned for so long.

Sleep deprivation was trying to win out. Despite the long, obsessive hours of writing, Joni felt that a catharsis of sorts was at work for Karl. Sometimes he would show her what he wrote, or read portions to her, but often he would not. He copied some notes over, almost all of what he had written was copied over at least once, and Joni would go through the throw-aways to see where his head was taking him. She so wanted to understand this process, and more than that, she wanted to be able to explain what was happening to his parents. She felt that if she could only bridge the gap between them, that some real progress could be made. How else could they truly know what was going on with their son?

Her letter of January 19th read:

Donald & Elaine:

I've retrieved some of Karl's notes from the trash. He tends to write on one pad then transfer to notebook paper.

Above all else, I think you can see, he is very confused. He definitely is moving toward health in writing these things out - and re-writing and reading them - but it's a painful process to watch.

The judge was very harsh with him yesterday - he told him that he needed to help himself - that no one else could do it - and that "the rest of the world is right - and you're <u>wrong</u>!" As an aside when he was done he said, "I'll see you again sometime." He obviously has no hope for Karl. Will talk to you soon.

One of Karl's pages that followed read:

Relationships

Ha! Here is a good one. Let me tell you, you only have one relationship - with God. Don't try to love any person. Learn to love the repetition of God's name, and he will reveal himself to you. He is much more eager than you can imagine. If you try to love a person, you will come to ruin. They will let you down. If you love God, then you will never let anyone down. On all sides, people will rely on you. Don't be sick.

Karl was now taking in massive amounts of coffee in an effort to try to stay awake. He feared sleep as the 'little death' that it is. Perfectionism taken to its most hideous extreme was blooming before her eyes, as Joni realized that his purpose was to be ever diligent, ever the good son (in terms of the Heavenly Father), and somehow, should he be good enough for long enough he would become the Chosen One. How common, she thought, for us to feel a degree of that at a given point in life....but this had no boundaries...this could lead to suicide or homicide perhaps if the belief was that such an action was the key to Righteousness. The seeds of War itself could be seen in this one man, devoted to good to the exclusion of reason. Irony flooded her heart - there   was something to be learned here - and how to recognize this within oneself was perhaps the greatest question. She was able to observe his actions and the destructive nature of his thoughts - but what about her *own?* Was she in fact helping this man? By trying to counteract his caffeine with herbs like valerian? By trying to reunite him with his family? What if his family was the reason why he had gotten to this point? What if his sleeplessness had actually kept him *alive?* Was she destroying her own life in favor of a futile exercise? Did she have any right to interfere? Wayne had said that he didn't believe we have the right to interfere with another life. Was he right? Was there any right and wrong? So many possibilities existed simultaneously in her

132

mind. One thing was certain…that she would never know for sure, unless at some point in the future Karl could achieve a level of happiness that seemed forever absent for him now. Even happiness is relative, though. She wondered if her idea of his best interests had anything at all to do with his own. Yet, through all of this, she had no choice. She had to support life the best way she knew how - and she only knew how from moment to moment. Books that she read, people that she talked to, helped, but fell short of the experience of just chanting and following her heart. Judgment loomed darkly in the back corner of her conscious thought, but she would have to deal with that later.

"I have to take down the cot in the living room," said Joni finally. "I just can't stand the clutter anymore." Karl had stopped sleeping through the night, pretty much. He would go to bed with Joni, then get up and write most of the night. Most times he would fall asleep in the living room chair. Her living room was only big enough for two overstuffed chairs and some side tables. The cot she'd borrowed was cumbersome and an eyesore in her cottage-like room.

"That's fine," Karl was in a cheerful mood, "I'm not sleeping any way."

"That's another thing I'd like to talk to you about, Karl. I have trouble sleeping with you up at all hours of the night. You can sleep with me if you choose, or you can have Kevin's room while he's not here. I need for you to sleep at night."

"I don't make any noise! I'm working! I'm not going to sleep! Never!" Karl's mood had shifted seamlessly. He got up and ran out of the house. Joni sat staring at the empty chair and joked to herself, "I think that went well…."

Joni's parents had the main house to which her little granny unit was attached. They were respectful of her privacy and trusted her. She had grown up away from them from the age of 18 to 37, but now rented from them for both convenience and support. Her dad had always been the authority, and it was only in recent years that she had overcome her fear of him – not that he was abusive, but as a child if he raised his voice she and her sister would run to their room crying. She couldn't wait to move out once she graduated high school and promptly got a room in town. He had said to her mother, "she'll be back." But until now, that was not the case.

Two days later Joni wrote to Karl's parents:

Dear Elaine and Donald:

Just another update! Karl seemed to be coming out of his anger on Friday evening. We've dropped the subject of the fine…He was trying to stay up all night again. He's over-diligent in his "work"…writing limericks, rhyming couplets and his dictionary.

Saturday evening we went to a party together…he enjoyed himself and did drink a glass of champagne for a toast. This helped to offset his caffeine intake. I've been able to slip some herbs into his cappuccino grounds to lessen the effects of the caffeine…he thinks I don't know that he's drinking it when he's up late at night.

On the way to the party he asked, "Do you really think my parents would listen to me now?" I told him yes and that I had talked to you on his behalf. He fears emotionalism, but I convinced him (maybe) that that's part of growing up…to be able to face your parents with compassion for their suffering, no matter how it's expressed. I still have a hard time when my dad yells at me, but finally I'm able to see that it's just his way of expressing feelings…since he was never allowed to do that.

After the party we went to bed and he got up a few hours later. We had talked about the fact that he wanted to shave his

134

head…he can never get his hair to look right…so I had told him to go ahead! I woke up when he came out of the bathroom with a ¾'s bald head!!! I helped him finish the job in the morning…but it really looks good…and should he decide to grow it back it shouldn't take too long either. He felt so accepted and loved and we joked a lot about his new "do" over the rest of the weekend. At one point he was just sitting and writing and he chirped, "I've got no Hair!!! Why didn't you tell me?"

Sunday night I went dancing and he didn't want to go. When I came home his mood had changed again. He had made himself a cappuccino and refused to come to bed. His writing seemed quite negative again, although I'm paying less attention to it. I feel that no matter what, the exercise of writing out his feelings is cathartic. I was annoyed, though, that he seemed to care little about the fact that I needed to go to work the next day and needed sleep. He really doesn't make noise, but it's still a disturbance to have him up all night. I gave in to sleep.

Monday morning he wanted to stay home, but I wouldn't let him. I don't want him to sleep during the day and then keep me up all night again. After work I picked him up. He was much more mellow, although we had a real manic session at dinner…rhyming and rhyming…..it's contagious, I joined in several times myself and tried to just enjoy the situation - if not, I'd probably go nuts myself! "Would you pass the butter, Please? I'd like to put some on my peas!"

"I'd love to do that for you, dear. To see you eat fills me with cheer." See what I mean?

I went to bed early and he came right in. He was very loving and trustful. I feel that we've made progress again in terms of intimacy, but he still clings to the idea that sex is bad- or that having sex somehow separates one irrevocably from God. I'm gently trying to counter this notion, without pushing him beyond

135

the boundaries of comfort. He may well live his entire life a virgin.

This morning he was still quite mellow and gentle; not his usual retreat after a close encounter, but that may come tonight. I share this with you (which may be awkward for a parent to read) only in terms of helping you understand fully the progress he seems to be making in terms of normal relationships. I think, too that the herbs are helping. We didn't take vitamins this morning, but he was quite sleepy already and slept almost the entire night. Will resume the regimen tomorrow...and his coffee is already laced with herbs should he decide to pull an all-nighter tonight. I hope he will be able to understand my motivation if he ever finds out...but it's a risk I feel I must take. Keep your fingers crossed and your prayers coming!

Love, Joni.

It was a routine now; Karl went out to shoot some hoops, or jump rope, or jog; she would nervously open the cappuccino maker with the coffee he had ready for later. He was continuously trying to deprive himself of sleep, but the very state that he felt was akin to enlightenment was destroying him both physically and mentally. Did she have a right to interfere? Was it a moral obligation? She only knew she had to try - right or wrong by anyone else's standards - and only her heart could lead her. Into the coffee grounds she would open a capsule or two of valerian, an herbal sleep remedy. She had been to the health food store and been shown several sleep remedies, she chose one with several herbs, but a predominance of valerian. Did it work inside the coffee grounds to reduce the impact of the caffeine? She had no way of knowing. Possibly not. It was a way to get it into him. As much as he tried to avoid sleep, she was becoming obsessed with the idea that sleep itself would be the miracle cure for what ailed him, but she was only partly right.

136

Dr. Apostle called to tell her that he would send a note to the judge saying that Karl needed medication and was psychotic. The problem was, he would have to get into more trouble for that information to be of much use. But, more trouble was right around the corner. It was just a matter of time before it reared its ugly head, of this he was certain.

The Outreach psychologist, Claude, called to let Joni know that he, too, had talked to the courts and jail regarding Karl. He had been told that they would not give Karl any psychological help as long as he only committed minor offenses. – They needed something drastic enough for them to say, "He needs help."

The circle was unbroken. A more serious offense could mean the loss of Karl's life, yet his inability to function in normal society was obvious. He could get help if he would voluntarily seek it, but in order to do that he would have to be sane enough to know he needed help. More trouble could help him in that direction - or it could have a permanent and damaging effect. Surely a more serious crime would entail some amount of jail time. Then if he was determined to need psychological help - the experience of imprisonment, itself, could lead to disaster. He clearly fit into no neat category. Then, of course, does anyone? It was a rude awakening, indeed, to see that as a society we hold no provision for such a person. We try to ignore them, as Joni knew she had herself. Never again would she be able to see a person walking along with a backpack without wondering if he or she was homeless. Never again would she think that highly intelligent people lived problem free lives. In fact, she was learning that many of the highly intelligent have major problems with psychosis.

But, scariest of all was the fact that never again would she feel that she was removed from the possibility of her own insanity. She knew she understood this man far too well for someone unschooled in psychology. She knew that she *had* to, but she did not know why. Perhaps she never would.

"As for me, you must know that I shouldn't precisely have chosen madness if there had been any choice."

- Vincent Van Gogh, 1889, in a letter to his brother

Chapter Seven - Descent

Karl seemed unable now to stop stealing. Joni had tried to convince him to take back the Christmas gifts, but was reluctant to push the issue due to his sincerity and sensitive nature. He was alternately easily bruised and ferociously arrogant. False bravado did not mask his pain, even though it could be hugely irritating and at times infuriating to Joni. She was learning to pick her battles with him, but she was losing ground. On the other hand, another arrest for shoplifting would put Karl back in front of the judge. This might become a blessing in disguise with more psychologists' recommendations now fattening his file. But adding felony counts to his rap sheet could damage his future, too. A dilemma, indeed.

"Now don't take anything today, Karl. I mean it," she would say. "I have to do what God tells me," he'd reply. Sometimes he'd come home with no coat. "God told me to give it away," he'd say.

Sometimes he'd have pens or pencils and paper that he'd say he bought. Joni gave him money almost weekly, so she wasn't quite sure of the veracity of that statement.

Karl would visit the library and "borrow" books. The problem was, he didn't have a library card, nor would they issue him one without an address. Joni wanted to help him, but he didn't want her help in this regard.

He befriended some college students and got passes into the campus library where he could work on the computer. This set up a whole new desire in him. He started to demand that Joni get her computer (a relative dinosaur) fixed so that he could use it.

She wanted to, but was unable to come up with the money, plus the dollars would be better spent on a new machine. Above all, if he was not willing to get a job or get help of some kind, she did not want to encourage him to think that he need only write pronouncements of his own grandeur to make it so. Having an available computer might only prolong the evasion of reality. But, because he was now writing in her newly covered living room chairs and falling asleep with pens in his hands and marking up the fabric, she decided it was time to make a concession. She rearranged a few things and set up a small desk for him in the living room.

"I've made a new place for you to write," she offered gently as he came in one evening. I thought it might be more comfortable for you, plus you won't get ink on my chairs anymore!"

He was touched. He sat down at the desk and ran his hands over the small white surface. A look of joy and peacefulness swept through him and out his eyes.

"Wonderful!" He exclaimed in his quiet tone. "Thank you!"

She felt pleased and a bit relieved. Her best intentions might not be understood, she feared, but this was one time when things were going right.

"Do you have a board or something like stiff cardboard?" was his next question. "Well, let's see - how big does it need to be - and what will you use it for?"
"Not too big - but big enough to tape this paper onto it," he said as he pulled out an artist's pad from his backpack.

"Oh," said Joni as she searched through closets and places where such a board might hide. "I know! I've got this board I used to cut out my quilt pieces - maybe that would work... or how about this thing that used to back a poster?"

"This would be just right!" Karl was holding up a brand new Airbake cookie sheet that Joni's mother had given her.

"That's new and rather expensive," she hesitated. "How about the old one?" as she pulled it out of the cabinet.

"That will do just fine," he said gratefully. "I'm going to paint a picture tonight. God wants me to paint His picture."

"Fine," Joni was curious as to what God might look like to Karl. "I'll start dinner," she continued as she left him alone for his now traditional 15 to 20 minutes of quiet time before dinner. As un-domesticated as she had become in recent years, Joni loved the routine of preparing his dinner and sitting with him and sharing tea almost every night. Perhaps it was a need long suppressed because her son was no longer living with her. She had lived alone for over three years now. Even though it cut into time she usually spent on other things, the ritual of their co-habitation had brought out a deep joy within her. Parts of her creativity she thought had long ago died off were resurfacing. *If he was only well,* she thought so many times. *I could easily be with him; our temperaments are so in line!* In truth, they got along famously, except when the Terrors began to take him over and he'd lapse into a paranoid confusion. Joni wasn't able then to reach him, he would become super arrogant and the look in his eye would change from loving and respectful to bitter hatred laced with fear. She knew at those times that he would see her as the devil, although he tried to play it cool. It was obvious to her that playing he was. She could almost hear the conversations in his head, "don't look at her...she's a temptation and if you give in to temptation - you know what happens. She doesn't really care about you - what do you think is going on when you're not around? After all, she's a woman, isn't she? You know that they are inferior creatures..."

But, for now, all was quiet and happy. She prepared dinner as he wrote. Music played softly in the background. They both enjoyed that. Presently she heard the slider open and he had gone out - just to the woodpile to gather fuel for tonight's fire. She loved it when he built a fire. He was proud of his contribution, too, because he knew she wouldn't bother with it on her own. He liked to see her happy - this was a relatively new and unexplored feeling for him. He hadn't been much on pleasing others for most of his 31 years, but something about this woman - when the Terrors were silent at least - something about her had made him want to please her.

One night he sang along with Rod Stewart, "...someone like you makes it hard to live without somebody else. Someone like you makes it easy to give, never think about myself..." It had been a more than precious moment for Joni. His sweet sincerity was something she would never again encounter, of that she was sure. And, though she was 'acting' as if she would marry him someday, the lines between reality and fantasy were blurring and running together in spots. This was one of those spots.

In the morning Karl presented her with the work he had done. By the fact that the paint was still wet, Joni surmised that it had been done recently, in the wee hours of the morning. A sun ball above a happy face and directly beneath that, a sad face, which topped a blue, repeating circle shape. From the lower left corner there was a white beam, which split in two just as it arched between the two faces and descended downward toward the right side of the painting. The background had been added after the fact, and was black with flecks of white stars.

The faces represented Gods according to Karl, and the sun was the Supreme God of all gods and the Universe. Joni knew what he wasn't explaining outright, though. The whole scene showed the happiness of the face near the sun 'god' and the unhappiness near the earth (blue circles). He was surely divided between heaven and earth - and was feeling downright negative about being earthbound, for sure. It made sense to Joni. Most everyone has those feelings at times. She wondered aloud if perhaps he might be able to sell his work and make a living that way. He wasn't interested. He didn't want to earn money.

Why should he, she thought…he's getting by okay without it. But what she said was,

"You may need it to buy more art supplies and to pay for food and stuff." She dropped the subject when she felt the wall between them get cold and thick. *Another time to pick that battle*, she thought.

Time was moving along with or without progress in the situation. Maybe this was all there was? She couldn't quite believe that, but then, her vision of a healthy life for him seemed almost laughable.

"Come over here, I have to tell you something," Karl was speaking gently and he pulled Joni onto his lap. "I don't know how to tell you this, but God doesn't want us to get married."

"Oh, that's okay, I understand," Joni was hoping there was the right mixture of disappointment and acceptance in her voice. "I'm going to put this ring in my jewelry box and keep it always." She kept her relief well hidden. Bullet dodged.

Karl seemed happy with her response. The matter was closed - at least for a time.

Joni chanted for Karl and envisioned him soaked through and through with her daimoku so that he'd heal. In the morning as she did her prayers Karl watched as he sat at the kitchen table sipping tea. As she finished and got up to grab her things before leaving for work he said to her, "You know I have this permanent vision of you in my head chanting. I hear it all the time." Joni smiled. It was good to be seen that way.

But that night Karl's mood had shifted again. He read to her his latest work which said that "you must go away from happiness, especially when you've been soaked and soaked in it." It struck Joni, because she had never used that visualization with her chanting - it was clear the effect had been felt. Her daimoku had soaked him - even though he still wanted to escape from the 'happiness' it brought him.

The next night Karl was not at his appointed pick-up spot after work. He had been in a very depressed state that morning - he had asked again for Joni to pay his fine and she had refused.

Joni's antennae told her that he was inside the mall, so she parked her car and stormed in. Up the escalator and directly to the food court – where he sat writing. She went over to him and asked if he was coming home. At first he just ignored her and then he looked up and said, "I want a computer and I want you to pay the $75.00 or I'm not coming home."

"Karl, I'm <u>not</u> paying your fine! I didn't steal anything. I don't have the money to fix my computer. Do you want to come home now or not?" She was fuming.

He shook his head no.

"FINE!" she said as she stormed back out of the mall. I've had enough of this was all she could think…but then, she remembered - she'd have to tell his parents.

"You did the right thing," said Elaine supportively.

"I can't take any more of this," cried Donald. "I'm on antidepressants now!" He wailed. The situation had clearly taken its' toll.

"Yes you can!" chirped Elaine. "We have to - we're expecting a miracle! Joni, you let us know what happens, won't you?"

"Of course, I'm afraid it's just a matter of time before he gets picked up for shoplifting again…"

"That's what I think, too," Donald replied with resignation in his voice. "But as we've all said before, that may be the only way he gets help!"

"I'll keep you posted," Joni mustered some slight courage, "it's not over, yet….we can still win!"

"Let's hope so," they said almost in unison.

Joni wrote a few days later,

Dear Donald & Elaine:

Well, it's Sunday morning - no word from Karl. I'm resisting the temptation to look for him. He must face the charges and stop trying to make others responsible.

Even though I know that his brain isn't functioning 100% properly, I feel that by dealing with his own challenges he can become stronger and gain self-respect. I see his maneuvering to make me pay his fine as a self-destructive course. If I did pay the fine he would again be powerless as a man. I think even in his seething over the fact that "Eve" refused to "help" him, he is respectful/fearful of her strength. I want so much for him to experience his own capability - but it can only come through acceptance of his responsibility.

Enough philosophy. Am sending along some photos (the last taken of him *with* hair- none yet of his new 'bald' look)

Also - he left a lot of writings behind - I'm sending what I see as most significant for now - it should all help if we ever do get him to treatment.

Interestingly I've had a book called Sexual Personae, for some time now - decided to pop it open and there is a bunch of discussion of Blake's work and his inability to come to terms with sex. It all gets very esoteric and heavy, but I find it coincidental to say the least that Karl is so drawn to Blake. (The book covers others, too, but calls Blake "our greatest poet of sexual anxiety" p286)

Who knows?

Anyway, I continue to pray with confidence that this will come full circle this year!

I keep envisioning Karl as a professor speaking happily at a podium. His sense of humor overriding all of his trials - and his inner strength a source of encouragement.

146

I know he is fighting a tremendous mental battle right now - we can only keep reassuring him and expect him to make it! (Like friends at the Finish Line as he races)
Thanks again for your support!

Love, Joni

Joni could feel Karl willing her to find him. She was hooked in beyond logic and reason - and went on her lunch hour to talk to him. She was running on the instinct of a hound dog...and her car seemed to know where to go, too. At the college with a little help from some sunning students, she found the way to the cafeteria. Toward the back, in a separate section, she found Karl half sleeping, half pretending to read. He looked dirty and gaunt. Unlike she had ever seen him before. As she approached he looked up with surprised disgust, but she noticed that her phone number was written on the back of his hand in red ink. She did not comment on it- best to pass on that one.

"Karl, would you like to come home and eat?"

He shook his head 'no', - his usual gesture in times of disgust. She saw real pain in his eyes, mixed with anger.

"You must be hungry," she continued. "Why don't you come home and at least eat and take a shower. You don't have to stay if you don't want to."

"I'm fine," he said and then slowly said, "Yes. God says I can go."

As he rose he steadied himself on the table. Frail was too kind a word for the way he looked. His pants hung on his hips as if draped over a cardboard cutout of a man.

147

His hair had sprouted in patches on his otherwise shaven head and a faint beard cropped out in splotches. It was clearly a chore to be awake, his eyes hung vacant as if lost in his skull.   A star school athlete reduced to this. Joni once again felt her heart break. It broke for him and for the suffering his parents endured, to see their son choose this wasting was incomprehensible. Yet, she knew that they were combing through stacks of memories, trying to figure where they had gone wrong. She was back to square one - or was it minus something by now? Had she maintained the progress she'd made, or had she slid back beyond the point of her beginning in this nightmare?

She wrote again - almost a compulsion now, to his parents:

Feb 2, 1994

Dear Donald & Elaine:

I'll probably be speaking to you before you get this letter, but I want to chronicle the events in writing. Here's the latest:

Yesterday at lunch time when I found Karl he agreed to come home for dinner and a shower and I told him I'd pick him up after work at the mall. I told him not to take anything (steal). When I picked him up he had a box of shoes. I told him to leave the shoes, but he refused and got into the car. I was in a red zone, so I allowed this, but told him I simply would not pick him up again if he had "stuff". When we got home I told him not to bring the shoes into the house.

He sat in the car for a while, lacing the shoes. The next thing I knew he was gone. I went out to the car…he had taken all of his things (backpack, coat and the shoes) with him. I got into the car to drive & look for him, knowing he couldn't have gotten far, but when I didn't see him down the road, I knew he was either still hiding in the trees or was determined to stay hidden

148

on a back road for a while. I came back home and several minutes later he appeared. Said he had gone for a walk. The shoes were gone. I knew he had ditched them somewhere nearby.

I made dinner for him, but I had explained on the ride home that if he wouldn't sleep he'd have to go back out on the street because I couldn't have him up in the house all night. He ate a very large dinner, stopping at times, because I'm sure his stomach has shrunk. He told me that he had lost 2 lbs. I said that wasn't bad for what he'd put his body through the last 3 days.

He did shower before dinner and shaved. At dinner he talked fairly pleasantly and asked how Kevin was, etc. Other than that he made no attempt to really connect with me. At one point he told me that he wrote the Book of Job (in another life). I laughed and said that most of us feel that way. It just struck me funny, knowing what you've been through!

In the car I told him that if he refuses to sleep his body will eventually give out and that he will end up in an institution. I told him that I could help him and keep anyone from harming him, but that I needed his cooperation. No response.

He had spent the night at Lyons Restaurant - they're open 24 hours. He had apparently been there the day before, too, because I found his check in the trash can. Its date/time stamped 1/30/94 5:47AM. He had french fries and coffee.

He did confess that I was right about the first night. He had taken a swan dive, (meaning he had fallen asleep), but said that since then he'd been up and felt fine. His eyes were somewhat bloodshot, but his skin coloring looks pretty good. He also said that he was "starving" when I found him...which he was. He was eating a small bag of corn chips and barely chewing.

149

At dinner he drank a whole pot of tea (herbal) and stated that he was so thirsty he could drink a river. Most likely he isn't getting enough water into his system, along with everything else.

After dinner I did gongyo (evening prayers) and he put on his headset, (a newly stolen radio) and laid flat on the floor. It must have felt like heaven to lie flat…even for a short while. He was trying not to hear my prayers, though.

I again asked if he would consider sleeping. He said no, so I told him he'd have to go back out. He was angry, but controlled. He gathered most of his clothes and put them into a paper bag. Then he asked for his writings. I told him that I had gotten rid of them. (I have them here at the office) He took his writing materials, but left behind his paints and most of his books. There was only so much he could carry.

I took him into town.…

Joni drove biting her tongue. She didn't want to cry. The radio was on softly. As she pulled into the parking lot of the coffee house she noticed Karl looking at her with the irony of the song that played, "I've still got her number, but I can't reach her anymore. I can't reach out and touch her heart the way I did before…" with a slight huff he got out of the car and carried his two grocery bags of belongings into the coffee shop.

Her letter continued…

I told him that he was welcome to come and eat any time and that he could call me if he wanted to talk. Carrying his stuff into the coffee shop must have been a humiliating experience, but lately he seems to thrive on that.

Anyway, he'll have to break through this time himself. I know he was close to calling me, because he had my phone number written on his hand. Unfortunately, his arrogance was only fed by my finding him first.

The sweet, unassuming, gentle nature that I originally saw in him is now hiding behind a self-centered, stubborn, arrogant veil. I know that both parts are extremes of his true self. Maybe they can meet somewhere in the middle to form a normal human being.

If you decide to kidnap him, I feel I can find him almost any time. Otherwise, I think he'll be picked up again soon for shoplifting as his activity in that area seems to be accelerating. If we're lucky he'll get delirious and do something crazy enough to warrant psychiatric help. In the meantime, know that you've done all you can and that there will be a happy ending eventually. I won't ever give up that dream.

Love, Joni

They had talked over the possibility of coming out and actually kidnapping their son off the streets of Santa Rosa. It certainly seemed like a viable alternative at this point, but there was always the chance that Karl would skip town or be unlocatable for long periods of time. The whole process was dragging along at a deadening pace. Joni was now far from the original thought that they would just get him on a plane and back to Minneapolis as soon as he was found. She wanted to help them, but had she helped too much? She thought that by letting them know the details of his life and writings they would be able to enlist psychiatric help. But she was learning that they were fragile themselves. They were weary and though they were thankful for her help, it was easier to let time pass a little between the crises.

One of the things she didn't tell them was that Karl had thrown his new hat away.

One of his recent writings had suggested that he take it off and stomp on it – because, she guessed, it represented ownership of material things. She had expected it would happen, but it still hurt a little.

Donald wrote back to Joni:

3 Feb 94

Joni:

We've Xeroxed some things. Some page from a new genetics book I received. The other is from the book by Patty Duke (Someone loaned it to Elaine). Karl doesn't seem to fit either bipolar disorder or schizophrenia perfectly, but has to be there somewhere.

If he would only allow help. I read somewhere that other people work on them 'til they finally agree. Who knows? It can't go on forever, can it? It's hard to think about how he used to be. I see his unicycle hanging in the garage and see his skiing equipment. Can still see him enjoying those things. Every time I go hunting and fishing there is a void. He used to love those activities so much. His old tackle box has been pretty well raided by Jeff and Dave, but the cherry rod his grandfather gave him is still here. Wish you could have seen him on downhill skis. He was outstanding! Can you imagine him pole vaulting 14 feet? Sometime look at how high that is. He still holds the high school record here.

If you want, tell him about his Dad being named the Best Undergraduate College Professor in Minnesota for this school year. I don't know if it would help or not. We miss the Karl we once knew so much.

Maybe try to get him to call us and ask for help. Be better to pay the $75.00 now before it goes up by $143.00. If he would just talk to Claude and consent to help.

The book says they do not want to give up their feelings and delusions - makes them superior.

Our love,

Elaine and Donald

Even though letters were flying back and forth between them, Joni and Karl's parents needed to talk about the situation. There were endless speculations and possibilities. Joni was convinced that there was some sexual abuse of some kind. Elaine and Donald had quite naturally resisted the idea, but on this morning Donald called to talk about just that.

"Joni, I've wracked my brain over the sexual abuse question - and although neither Elaine nor I could come up with anything, there was an incident years ago I thought I'd run by you. Karl was at Bible camp for a week and when we went to pick him up he came running up to us crying and pointing to his mouth. The camp counselor said Karl had hit his mouth on the bed a few days before. He actually lost a tooth and had clearly been injured. The counselor was very haughty and arrogant about it and we sued because we had not been notified of the problem when it occurred. It was a very ugly scene. We won, though, and that's how Karl got his college fund."

"How old was he at the time?"

"I think he was 7 or maybe 8? I can look it up for you. What do you think?"

Joni felt like a piece of the puzzle had fallen into place. Something about this incident smelled real bad. "Donald, I think this is it. Why would Karl hit his <u>mouth </u>on a bed? It doesn't make sense. And the fact that he came running to you crying, even though the incident had been over for a few days seems suspect also. Who else was there? Is there anyone you can ask about this now?"

"No, the Pastor who ran the camp has long since retired. He's in Texas now, I think.

I doubt that he had anything to do with it, but now that we're talking about it, he <u>did</u> come and apologize three times. I thought it was a little odd, but never connected anything. Here the counselor who was responsible (supposedly accidentally) was not at all remorseful, but the pastor came to apologize three times!"

"I've got chills over this, Donald. It sounds like truth to me."

"I don't know, Joni. Elaine doesn't believe it could have happened…" Donald hesitated.

"We may never know for sure, but I really do think there is something traumatic that happened to Karl - even with the separate onset of schizophrenia - something else is going on with him around sex. He's terrified on some level."

"Well, I hope he gets treatment soon. It seems as though they give lithium salts for both schizophrenia and bipolar disorder from what I've read."

Joni was nodding; she had read the same thing. "What I don't get is what does it matter then which diagnosis he has - if the treatment is the same!"

"Exactly what I've been thinking," Donald agreed. "Guess I'd better get going, Joni.

154

Thanks so much for all you're doing. I'll send you some money to help pay for groceries."

"Thanks, Donald," Joni was simultaneously remembering her first phone encounter with him. She had felt intimidated by his Ph.D. status; thinking he was somehow more powerful than she by virtue of that and the fact that he was the parent of this man-child. Nothing could have been further from the truth. He was warm and sensitive; a caring man, controlling perhaps, but down to earth nonetheless. Elaine, too, was very warm toward Joni, but she had the veil of religion about her at all times. Joni's perception of it kept her at a cautious distance with regard to her own spiritual practice. Still, there was something deeper going on there. Elaine was never able to talk to Joni without Donald on the other line. Yet, Donald was home on sabbatical, so he often called when she was not home. An unasked question began to form in Joni's mind. What was it that Elaine *really* wanted to say?

Time seemed to compress and become more valuable each day. The strain was on- Who would win? Would a strait jacket be the only way out? Would he end up in jail forgotten by 'The System', even farther from the help he needed? Would they give him shock treatment? How horrible a thought - would it make him better, or worse? The clock was ticking quietly away.

Another lunch hour had come. Joni had to find Karl again and try to mend the chasm between them - for his own sake. But she knew it would not go easily. It was her birthday, though - so maybe she'd get lucky today. The air was crisp and clear as she got out of her car on campus. She was feeling way too conspicuous in the full length royal purple coat she had bought on sale last summer. She had been waiting for some cooler weather just to enjoy it - but it was like a neon light and she wanted to blend in. *Oh, well,* she thought, *I'm here now - if he sees me coming and runs - there's not much I can do. I hope he's here!*

She glided in to the cafeteria. Karl was there and pacing the outer perimeter of the room. She walked up to him and said, "Hi."

He ignored her and continued to pace. She followed. He changed direction. She followed.

"I want to talk to you, Karl," she insisted.

"Leave me alone," he said as he changed direction again and angrily walked away. Joni kept up with him. "How about some lunch?" she asked. No answer came.

"Aren'tyou hungry or thirsty at least?" By now Joni was aware of the comic scene she was playing out on this unlikely stage. All eyes in the cafeteria were on them. The six foot tall bald skeleton followed by the five foot tall purple from head to toe gliding thing. She could hardly keep from laughing, herself, but she was determined to talk to him.

"Stop following me," said Karl again…with slightly less resolve. His pace was slowing. He was becoming confused as to what to do next.

"I'm not going to stop until you sit down and at least have a drink with me," said Joni firmly.

Karl stopped. The thoughts ran over his brain and registered each footprint in his eyes. He was computing again. "Okay," he conceded, "I'll have something to drink."

They went to the counter and each got iced tea. Joni paid, reluctantly because he still refused any food. He led her to the table where he had left his books. And she started with

156

her usual questions, "Are you doing okay? Have you been eating?"

Silence held for minutes that seemed to fill the room. "I'm going to be on TV," he said brightly. He had snapped into his other mode.

" Oh, really?" said Joni - thinking to herself - you may well be, but not for the reasons you're thinking.

"Yes! I have a meeting with the people at the Press Democrat. I'm going to tell them all about who I am."

"So, you have an appointment?" Joni wanted to see how far he'd take this line.

"Yes. This afternoon." Karl was looking down now as he talked.

"What time?" asked Joni pressing further.

"I…I can't remember right now, I have it written down."

"Karl, you know that isn't real…" she went way out on a limb…"why don't you try to sleep. You'll feel much better."

Karl glared at her. He was furious at the suggestion. But, as he glared, she looked him straight in the eyes, and sent him a look of pure truth and love. Briefly, it came over him; she glimpsed the recognition and the longing in his eyes. He couldn't hold his stare and looked away, now softened and in pain. She slipped a $10 bill across the table to him and he accepted gingerly, then got up with a jerk and began pacing the room again. Joni sighed at she got up to leave and walked up to him as she left.

"You know, Karl, today is my birthday, so I wanted to thank you for having a drink with me."

"Oh, Happy Birthday," he said gently, but continued his pace and looked away as soon as the words left his lips. The purple thing glided out the door and back to work.

2/8/94

Dear Donald & Elaine,

Your daily report! Karl is looking okay as we discussed. I gave him $10 today - will try to connect with him again in a day or two, but he's still quite angry with me. Inside I know he does want to connect, but it's tough getting through.

After talking about the incident at Bible camp, I am even more convinced that Karl was indeed abused. I'm playing junior psychiatrist again - sending you more of his writings. Some of it may be duplication, but bear with me.

He is definitely fighting a return to a "normal" life - perhaps memories are returning? At any rate, he is still in the area - still approachable and, I feel, in better psychological shape than he was in December - if only due to the "connection" with me. The fact that he doesn't dance any more is worrisome, but he's trying to blend in with the students right now. This will be hard to maintain during the summer months when fewer people attend college. Also, as we discussed, if he becomes too noticeable, campus security will kick him out. I fear he's already been kicked out of local restaurants, etc. - since he told me when he was on the streets (in Petaluma) he had to constantly remember which places he couldn't go.

I'm feeling a bit drained mentally and emotionally today - work has been stressful, too - but will continue my 3 hour a day campaign of chanting for him. I was able to look him directly in

158

the eyes and he couldn't stare me down no matter how many times he tried - he'd look at me with anger, but it would soften and he'd have to look away each time.

I'm dashing this off (again) sorry for the mistakes, etc.

Love,
Joni

She went dancing that night and got lost again in the joy of music and movement.

Back home, she pulled off her cowboy boots and flopped into bed. The morning would be easy; it was the weekend at last.

The next morning the phone rang.

"Hello, Joni, this is Elaine." Joni listened to the almost whispering voice on the other end of the line. She was in the middle of tearing her bed apart to wash the sheets. It was one of her favorite ways of venting frustration - to rip the sheets off in a frenzy. Putting fresh ones on afterward in an afterglow of next-to-godliness, she was caught off guard by the call. Elaine sounded different, like she was about to let loose. Joni felt a wave of tension - she's going to tell me that Karl is an ax murderer, she thought. The Twilight Zone is about to reach its snappy, but ironic conclusion. She sat down on the bed to brace herself.

"There's something I want to tell you," the voice continued and then broke into a sob.

"What is it, Elaine?" Joni asked, now feeling sympathetic, but still guarded.

"I couldn't tell you while Donald was around, but I think I know what happened to Karl."

"Okay, Elaine, take your time, I'd really like to hear what you have to say."

"I feel like I can talk to you, Joni, even though we've never met. "The truth is, there was something wrong with Karl when he was in the third grade. He teacher told us he was withdrawn, but in those days no one went to psychologists. He never did <u>anything</u> wrong and always got straight 'A's, so we just never did anything about it. But, Joni, Donald pushed him so hard. Every night the first words out of his mouth to Karl were, 'How high did you jump today?' or 'How fast did you run?' He'd never even say 'Hello' first before he started in on Karl. Karl became so driven it was scary. He would jump over and over and over again. Even when his coach told him to stop, he wouldn't. He just drove himself to the point of exhaustion. His father never praised him; he never just spent time with him. He's really an ogre. I hate to say it, but it's true. Then when Karl was 17…." Elaine started crying again.

"It's okay, Elaine," Joni ventured.

"No, I want to tell you this, "she continued as she pulled herself together. "When Karl was 17 he found out that his father was having an affair. He had picked up the extension phone and overheard them talking. Donald was having an affair with one of his students. It just devastated Karl. He found out his idol had feet of clay. Naturally I was devastated, too. Joni, ours has not been a good marriage. Too make matters worse, Donald wouldn't face the kids without making an excuse for his behavior. He made me confess to them that I wasn't a virgin when we got married. Karl took Donald's side. Justifying his actions, because I had been with another man…so I have to admit, I became distanced from Karl. Jeff, his brother became my friend and defended me. So, you see, I may have driven

160

Karl away - I just couldn't get close to him after I saw the way he judged me."

"What a cowardly thing to do!" Joni was enraged by Donald's action and mortified at the mental picture of a mother confessing a 'sin' in total humiliation to her own children. What a horrible scene that must have been...how could she even do it? She should have told him to go to hell - but, shame is a powerful weapon. It made her sick to think about it. Elaine had won the prize of her husband, but was it a prize worth winning?

"Elaine, I don't think Karl's illness is your fault. I'm sure that the whole thing was a nightmare for the family, but I really don't believe that that alone would have caused Karl's illness. You said, yourself, that he had had some problems as early as the third grade. Please don't blame yourself..." She hoped that her voice was reassuring. She wasn't quite sure what to do with the bombshell of information she had just been handed. "Elaine, what made you stay?" was all that came out of her mouth.

"I guess I just decided that I loved Donald enough to stay married. But I'll tell you one thing; I'm not putting up with any more crap! When he tried to break the affair off with the woman, she became obsessed and wouldn't let go for the longest time. I'm telling you, we went through hell over that one! But, Joni, I'm only telling you all of this in case it can somehow help Karl. I feel like he might say or do something and you would know better why he's acting the way he does with this background information. I knew that Donald would never tell you about it."

"Elaine, I admire your courage. I feel honored that you've entrusted me with this information. There is one question that I have to ask, however, and that is 'did Karl ever witness any domestic violence?'"

"What do you mean?"

161

"Did Donald ever hit you? I'm asking because I need to know if there's a possibility that Karl could get violent with me."

"No. Nothing like that ever happened." Elaine answered calmly and clearly which greatly relieved Joni.

"Okay, good," Joni sighed. "That's good. And, Elaine, please feel free to call me anytime you want to talk."

"Thank you for helping Karl and we'll talk again soon. I love you!"

"I love you, too, Elaine. Us mothers have to help each other, don't we? Okay, I'll talk to you soon, bye."

The bed got made somehow, but Joni didn't remember doing it. Were these pieces of sky or did they go to another puzzle all together? At any rate, it felt like a weird kind of progress was being made. And so it was - Karl called the next evening.

"Hi, it's me." Karl sounded cheerful and bright on the phone. "I thought maybe we could try again. I think it's okay if I sleep a little bit."

"Okay, as long as you know the rules, I'll pick you up after work. Do you want to meet at the mall?"
"Whatever is convenient for you - I could try to walk over there, but don't know if I could make it by five..."

"No, no. The mall is fine - you can't walk clear over here by five. I'll see you there." "Okay, thanks. I'll be waiting outside. Thanks again!"

Joni hung up the phone with mixed emotions. Would he actually sleep and work toward health? She was growing weary

162

of the game. In earlier months she would have jumped on the phone to call his folks with the hope-filled news, her voice brimming with positive emotion, but now, she decided to wait and see for a bit. The thought of giving up completely hadn't really occurred to her. She still felt there was more to do - but what? Most of all she wondered how long it would take. Her earlier resolve to see things through was thinning like lake ice at the end of winter.

Karl was at his appointed place at the appointed time with bells on, so to speak. He jumped into the car and gave Joni a kiss. "Hi! I missed you!" he said as if nothing had happened the day before. Joni wanted to bring him around to reality just a smidge.

"Did you have your meeting with the TV guys yesterday?", she asked.

"No. It didn't work out," he replied gingerly. "But you'll be with me when it happens…you can be famous, too," he encouraged.

"Karl, I'm not interested in being famous," Joni chose her words carefully, "It's you that I care about just the way you are. You don't need to go into Samadhi to impress me. I'd really like to support you to live a happy and fulfilled life." Then, changing the subject before the full weight of the inevitable silence could hit, she asked, "Do you have any special requests for dinner?"

"Anything is fine," he said as he draped his arm between the seats so that his hand just gently brushed her hair as she drove. He was in a good mood, but they both knew it wouldn't last.

Depression

"In addition to my other numerous acquaintances,
I have one more intimate confidant. . . . My depression is the
most faithful mistress I have known—no wonder, then, that I
return the love."

- Søren Kierkegaard (1813–55), Danish philosopher.

Chapter Eight　　　Depression

Karl's writings were almost completely dark now. Other than the fact that he had announced that he was William Shakespeare and William Blake in past lives, he kept conversation to a minimum. This was a bad sign. Joni found herself rummaging through his trash basket to see what he had written. Instinctively she felt that although he didn't share his work, he had left original copies intact for just that purpose. She knew she wasn't hiding anything from him, but direct confrontation about his subject matter was definitely out. A word or phrase said with conviction or the least hint of sternness would send him running out of the house returning anywhere from 30 to 60 minutes later with a rebuff, "You can't yell at me." She felt a mixture of curiosity at the way he perceived her speech and disgust at his behavior. More than once she thought it might be more humane to slap him upside the head rather than what she really did do- reason with him.

"You know, Karl," she'd say, "I wasn't yelling at you. I was just talking. I'm sure that you know the difference and that you've heard real yelling before." With that, she'd drop the subject and go about her business.

She continued to write his parents at least weekly and sent copies of his writings and paintings in hopes that someone, someday would be able to diagnose and treat him. An uneasy feeling about her own dishonesty had to be squelched - her single-minded purpose had to take precedence or all could be lost. She wasn't letting Karl in on the details that his parents were privy to. She was copying his works and sending them off to them behind his back.

She didn't know what else to do, but she couldn't back out now. It still felt important to her and she doggedly held the vision of his success in her head and her heart. It wasn't about her. It was about supporting the full potential of life. Right or wrong, she knew that judgment would follow her. Life is too short not to take risks, of this she was very sure.

Karl settled in to a routine of sleeping in the living room chair again. A shift in him had definitely evolved. He was eating well again, and had come to accept a small portion of the truth that his body needed rest. For over a week he slept between six and seven hours a night. He was spending less time at the mall now that the holiday shopping throngs had thinned out. His new hangouts became the library and a local health food restaurant. He left each morning after breakfast, even on weekends, to find his niche for the day. Joni was able to keep her life on an even keel because of it. She made her plans independent of him, but always kept in mind the necessity of his meals. She felt thankful that he was so independent that if she needed to be gone for the evening, he could stay out and fend for himself. She rarely let him stay in her home alone.

One Saturday as she vacuumed the floor, the phone rang. Karl hadn't been gone for more than an hour, but now sounded light and full of fun on the other end, "Hi! It's me! What are you doing?"

"I'm just vacuuming," she answered. "Where are you?"

"I'm at the library. It's such a beautiful day, though; I'm going for a walk. What are you doing tonight?"

"I'm planning on going dancing. You know you're always welcomed to come...you are my favorite dance partner."

"No, I don't think so..." Karl seemed put off. "You go ahead and have fun," he said reassuringly.

"Okay, well then I'll be home around 11:30 or so - do you have someplace to be?" "Sure - I'll either walk home or call you later and let you know where I am."

"Okay, fine...and if you change your mind, you know where I'll be!"

Joni hung up without any emotion one way or the other. Asking him to dance was a long shot, but she would go and have a good time anyway.

Thirty minutes later the phone rang again. "Hi! It's me again!" Karl was still cheerful.

"I've just found out that I can go! The dancing will be good for me. I just wanted to let you know that I'm on my way home, so don't leave without me."

"Great!" Joni was excited. For the moment it was like talking to a normal person again...although she wasn't sure how the evening would go. It didn't really matter; she was ready willing and able to take responsibility for her own good time - no matter what happened with Mr. Karl.

"I'm so glad you decided to come," she said to Karl as they jumped into the car. "Everyone has been asking about you - they'll be so happy to see you!" She was laying it on a little thick, but folks were always glad to see him - and she knew that Wayne would give him a boost for sure. They had a great time dancing. Wayne was supportive and talked with Karl like an old friend. Lots of people said "good to see you" and gave Karl pats on the back. When asked what he'd been doing he said, "I've been going to school." He wasn't lying. Joni just smiled and kept her mouth shut.

The night ended all too soon and when they got home Joni said to him as they came through the door, "Thanks for a nice evening!"

To her surprise he turned and quipped, "Yes! It was fun!"

The next day, however, the Terrors were back and he was being badly punished for having a good time. Back to black. Joni hated to be witness to his torment. It was obvious to her that it was all so unnecessary - but then, how much of what we each go through in life is unnecessary torment? She wanted to remember this as a touchstone for future reference. Too many times she had taken herself too seriously. She understood a part of Karl's pain and that scared her. Why was she so in tune with this crazy guy? Was she, herself, near some kind of invisible brink or did she just have a good memory from rougher times? It seemed to follow, no matter what questions she asked herself, that it all had a purpose - what, exactly, she didn't know just yet. It was too coincidental an experience not to have some grand design; whether Karma or God or Physics didn't much matter.

168

Joni's best course of action was to be a friend to Karl as best she could. This meant holding back on the nurturing that came to her naturally as a mother. The last thing Karl needed was another mother. His behavior in some ways seemed to be an attempt to manipulate her care and concern, but the double-edged sword of that manipulation was standing ready to cut her to ribbons. What was worse was the sword of self- deprecation that was flaying his soul by his own hand. She wanted to quiet the Terrors without raising the suspicions of any other personalities vying inside him.

Part of Joni's letter of 2/15 to 'the folks' read:

"...As we get closer to the 28th (the court date) I suspect he'll act out. He's thrown away his petty theft ticket and the failure to pay fine ticket was in my bedroom trash can. I feel it's most important that he learn to communicate about what is troubling him, and I don't want to be in a position to be acting like his mother rather than a friend.

He is now writing new things...I peeked...it seems to be a play about two young men in military school getting in to war. He's asked about history books and wants to know more. He's also very enthralled with his books about the universe and the stars, etc. Last night I asked if he would ever consider going back to school. He said no, but when I asked, "Not even for astronomy?" he said that he thought that might be interesting. I'm encouraged that his thirst for knowledge seems to be directed to new learning and thought...with a slighter emphasis on God and His directorial commands. The problem is, if he is as clear as I think he is mentally, he now faces the insurmountable truth that he is in a really bad place...no friends, no career, facing jail and desperate enough to have to live with me...which I'm sure makes him feel weak. His only hope is to ask for help...and I think that that is the most distasteful prospect of all. (I speak from my own stubborn experience)

Personally, I see that each time I begin to distance or let go, he senses this and comes back. He will not come as close as he once was, though. I am keeping my mind open, but feel that he may not be able to ask for or accept real help for quite some time.   In the meantime, I'm just enjoying my life...not dependent on his moods for my happiness. I know exactly how to handle the situation and as long as it feels okay to me I'll continue. If I meet someone else who wants to have a real relationship, things may change...but so far Karl is still the most special guy to me...even with his illness. I am doing what I can for him as a cause for my own son's happiness and as a cause for myself. In order to have this kind of treatment and care I feel I must learn how to give it. Either way, I win, because I'm doing what's in my heart.

Love, Joni

Joni opened her mail. Another card from Elaine and Donald. This one was so beautiful. A Loving valentine thanking her for her help with Karl. She cried as she read it - out of joy and out of pain. She knew too well that this could all end badly- and she wanted so much for their son to be returned to them. The real Karl needed to be restored, whether he was destined to remain in California or not was secondary. A second envelope held a packaged video tape for Karl and a valentine for him. "Your parents have sent a tape of last Christmas," Joni encouraged. "Would you like to watch it? It should have the whole family on it."

"Not right now," Karl was non-committal. Subject dropped. This was definitely one that she didn't want to push...because the possible range of reactions to his family was uncharted territory at this point. Would he be angry? Upset? Happy? Heaven only knew...and Joni was not at all sure whether the whole idea would be a help or hindrance to his health. The tape sat by the VCR and as days passed, it remained untouched.

In her letter of 2/17/94 Joni wrote:

Dear Elaine & Donald,

Thanks so much for the beautiful valentine. It made me cry. We still have not viewed the tape. The other night when I brought it home Karl said he'd have to think about watching it and I haven't pushed the issue. He may just decide to take a look.

He wanted to stay home again today, but I again used my father as the reason that he can't hang around the house. [Joni's father had definite ideas about who should be around the house. Even though she paid rent, Joni felt that it was fair. In fact, she was amazed that her father hadn't been more opposed to Karl being there.] Still don't have the nerve to say I don't feel right about him staying home relaxing while I'm out working.

He continues to stay in the living room chair at night and refuses to have any physical contact with me. It feels a bit odd because he used to like holding hands and hugging so much. He's pleasant, but the underlying tension is draining. He is sleeping at night…so that's a positive. I've been able to get his herbs into him regularly. He did a drawing last night intending to show the hierarchy of gods…he thinks this is a revolutionary idea, but it sounds like simple pagan philosophy to me. In fact, in Buddhism we do refer to 'gods', but these are just the protective forces in nature such as the moon, sun, etc., etc.

I have again retrieved some writings from the trash. Karl is terrified of feelings. I know that inside he is crying out for connection as we all do, but it gets harder and harder to live with him and not talk about real issues. The only way I can keep going now is to try and focus on this as a book that I will one day write. I actually care too much for Karl to effectively help him. I am learning so much about respect for human life. My own selfish nature, however, vies for more attention. Keep praying for me, I'll continue to chant…I'm still determined to see a happy ending. Sorry to be so wimpy in this letter…just want to be honest. This is a challenge for me.

Oh! Did see some words of encouragement recently in Reader's Digest by Charles

R. Swindoll: *"Courage is not limited to the battlefield or the Indianapolis 500 or bravely catching a thief in your house. The real tests of courage are much deeper and much quieter. They are the inner tests, like remaining faithful when nobody's looking, like enduring pain when the room is empty, like standing alone when you're misunderstood."*
It reminds me of how much courage must really dwell inside Karl…for he is so misunderstood and can't find his way…yet he never gives up. What a brilliant gift he could give to the world if he could turn his strength toward health.

Love always, Joni

"Hello, Redwood Counseling Services, may I take a message?"

"Yes, this is Joni Mathews, I'd like to make an appointment with Judy Lovett, would you just tell her I need a tune-up?"

"Okay, sure. We'll have her return the call."

Joni hung up feeling a little lighter. It had been some time since she had seen Judy in counseling, but she liked to keep in touch and get a session every five or six months now.

"I've got an appointment from six to seven tonight," she told Karl as they drove home. It's right here in town, though, so I shouldn't be long."

"Where are you going?" he asked innocently.

"To see my counselor…I go every once in a while now, just to get straight," she replied with a cryptic kind of sideways glance. She was hoping he would feel her comfort in accepting the help of a psychologist. At the same time she was feeling a tinge of defensiveness, just in case he should razz her or make an untoward remark. He didn't.

"Hi Judy!" Joni quipped as she entered the pink office. She had brought her warm coat as she and Judy were always cold in the office. There was someone else in the building that seemed to know how to manipulate the air conditioning to suit their own hot flashes. As a result, it tended to be winter all year, except on odd days, when the gods surprised them.

Joni wasted no time in explaining her latest adventure to Judy who was always unflappable. It was an amazing quality and one she was sure had to be learned well to be successful in the counseling business. When she was finished, Joni listened to Judy's summation of the session.

"What I hear is that although lots of good things are coming from you present situation, you are still basically not getting your needs met."

"Is that it?" Joni wondered out loud. "Of course, that's right." She startled herself with her own ignorance some times. What seemed so obvious did not come naturally to her. She had been so focused on the goal of Karl's health, that she had lost sight of her own needs. A simple truth, but one that she would have to face more than once before she caught on to the way out of it. "Thanks, Judy," she said as she hugged the slight

173

woman goodbye. "I'm sure I'll be seeing you again," she laughed. She felt stronger just for having had the time to think about her own course of action. She had definitely gotten her money's worth once again.

"I'm sure you will," said Judy warmly as she hugged Joni back. "How did it go?" asked Karl as Joni came in the door.

"Fine!" Joni said brightly. She was not going to discuss details, but felt glad that Karl had showed interest and concern. *Sometimes he just seems so normal* she thought to herself.

It was time to look at things with new eyes. Joni was a young single woman with a lot of love to give, but this was not the relationship she needed. What Karl needed far beyond her help at this point was psychiatric treatment, and she had no intention of being his psychiatrist. What she did realize, though, was that she was deeply attached to him and that that very attachment in and of itself might be a detriment to him at some point. Surely, it was a detriment to her, except during those times when she could rise above the everyday circumstance and look at the opportunity for growth she was experiencing. Which way to think? She drove herself nuts with her own thought processes. She thought about the Gosho (Buddhist writings) that said, "Become the master of your mind, don't let your mind master you." She was always trying to learn that one over and over. For a person who lives in their mind so much, this is difficult wisdom to grasp.

But as much as she wrestled with her own mind, she was witness to a battle royal ongoing in Karl's. He was trying again to avoid sleep at every chance. He was also successfully avoiding physical contact with Joni. Sex was out of the question, but because he had denied it so vehemently, it was now gaining an inordinate amount of his thoughts and energy. He would jog, skip rope or step on the alpine climber with determination. It was obvious to Joni that he was fighting off

174

his own needs and desires. His pain seemed deeper than fear to her. The worst of it was that she could not comprehend what he must be feeling and thinking. It was off the scale of any pain that she had known, and she had known plenty. Compassion sometimes felt like a warm blanket encircling her in easy fashion, but often, too, it was a bitter pill caught in her throat.

She longed for him to move toward wellness and she simultaneously resented that he now denounced his caring for her. She knew that he was using her, yet she didn't feel used at all, since she had asked for the trouble in her house.

Despite all of that, Joni saw changes brewing. It was now well past two months that Karl had been living with her - albeit with several absences. She began to sense a larger problem - perhaps Karl would only be able to connect with one of his parents at a time.

Donald and Elaine both cared deeply for Karl, but their approaches to that caring seemed more and more diverse. Elaine would enlist the help of prayer groups and colleagues were praying weekly for him, but basically, her life was going to go on and she was never going to give up. Donald, on the other hand, was on anti-depressants. He was torn apart by the whole process and in his pain Joni sensed a "stop-the-train-I-want-to-get-off" desperation. He could give up. He could face the end of either Karl or himself just to make the pain stop. He was certainly in Hell. Joni wrote and suggested that Elaine come to California for an extended visit in hopes that Karl would be able to connect with her and then move on from there. It was only a suggestion, but one that wasn't well received. It was also time for them to start talking to Karl on the phone -even though he had been avoiding that for a long time. Joni was ready to start pushing them gently.

Elaine and Donald were at first anxious at the prospect of talking on the phone with Karl. They weren't sure whether he would bolt once he knew that they could contact him at will.

They had walked on egg shells since their unsuccessful attempt earlier that year to bring him home with them. Karl was no longer the son they knew, but they knew he was inside this stranger somewhere. The unspoken fear between them was obvious even to Joni - what if he was gone forever? At this juncture, with progress being made in terms of Karl's ability to recognize his situation, it was downright scary to think that they could make a false move and blow the whole thing out of the water. They were walking on uncharted territory and they knew it.

"I'm fine."

Joni thought she heard Karl speaking through the bathroom door. "What?" she called out.

"Okay, thanks," he was hanging up the phone.

"Who was that?" she asked as she came out of the bathroom.

"My parents," said Karl without inflection.

"How are they?" she was going to go gently, but all the way to the 'Wall' that would end their conversation.

"They're fine." Karl walked away throwing the 'Wall" up behind him.

"I bet they miss you." she ventured anyway.

No response. The conversation had ended. *Jesus has left the building she thought to herself and chuckled.*

In the evening after dinner, Karl was feeling frisky again. "Let's watch a movie tonight!" He sounded happy and inviting, so Joni fell right in....

"Fine! Go ahead and pick one out and I'll join you when I finish the dishes." She was ready to get close again, but she wasn't going to be pushy about it. Karl was lying on the bed as she settled in on the opposite side. They were both fully clothed, on top of the covers and he commented about the movie. A violent scene emerged on the screen and Joni took the opportunity to cuddle close for his protection. "I'm scared!" she said smiling as she drew close to his arm.

Karl flew off the bed in a rage and stormed out of the room. He said nothing, but was obviously deeply disturbed by her touch. Joni felt like kicking herself. She had moved too fast, thinking things were normal again (as if they ever were). She followed him out to the living room where he sat staring. Without a word, she sat down and waited. She waited in silence, just knowing that she needed to be there and nothing more. She knew she was learning patience as 30 minutes and then an hour passed. As gently as she could she asked him if he was okay. Another 40 minutes passed and he was still scowling, not saying a word. It amazed Joni because she had expected that he would run out of the house and go for a walk as usual, but he didn't. She felt as though he wanted to talk, but couldn't - part of her felt that he was simply as confused as she was as to what had happened.

"I'm going to bed now, Karl," she said softly. "I'm sorry to have upset you, but I really didn't mean to. I hope that you will come to bed and rest." She dared not use the word 'sleep'. Then, quietly, after almost 2 full hours of silence, she went to bed to wait out the morning. Karl moved about busily in the living room just minutes after she left and within the hour he came to bed.

The next day they had planned on going to the Planetarium. When Karl got up he was ready with his plans for the day. He was going to the library and would be home for supper. Joni reminded him that he had wanted to go with her

177

to the Planetarium and that she was going to the 3 o'clock show. Karl hesitated searching the floor for an answer. He had forgotten, but felt like he should go to the library. Joni was miffed. She was going to do all of the housework while he went off to do whatever he wanted. Her feelings seemed to trip over themselves in somersaults. She would feel hopeful at his positive moods, then sad or angry at his arrogant silences, then she would feel compassion well up as she realized how difficult it was for him just to be in the world.

As he left she snapped that he was going to have to help around the house or get a job to contribute in some way. Karl left without a word - trying to outrun her words.

Fine! She thought. I'm going to do what I have to do and if he doesn't come home by the time I'm ready to leave, I'll just go - in fact, I think I'll go dancing tonight - I'll save the Planetarium trip and go with Shirlee. She was cleaning with a fury. It always made her laugh inside - I should get angry more often, she thought…that's when I do my best work! It was times like these that she most believed in a Creator, because she would think of how ridiculous she must look ripping her bed apart like her life depended on it. I'm merely a joke for the Universal Sense of Humor, she would think. Another fine mess you've gotten us into, Ollie. She burst into tears and laughter simultaneously as she pictured the whole Abbott and Costello routine a mere schizophrenic talking to himself. A life this weird <u>must </u>be entertaining to <u>someone</u>, she thought.

Three o'clock came and went. Joni got ready for dancing. As often happened, when the hour drew near to leave, she thought about changing her mind and just staying home. Sometimes that in itself was a luxury. But, at 4:15 the door suddenly slid open and in popped Karl. "We can still make the 5 o'clock show!" he quipped, his voice full of hope and animation. Joni was stunned.

"You want to go now?" She asked as if he was in mid conversation, rather than a newly materialized ghost. She felt her own inner tugging - 'don't go with him - go dancing by yourself - stay mad' - but it seemed silly to stay mad - especially if she had to conjure up an anger. It was six of one and half a dozen of the other at this point.

"Yeah, I'd really like to go…", Karl was staving off a wave of fear that his behavior had put him in the dog house.
Joni sensed it immediately and couldn't bring herself to chastise him. "Let's go!" she said and they were off in less than 3 minutes.

The show at the Planetarium was about Black Holes. Joni was entertained to her bones with the puns that ran through her head - If there was anything so intensely dense that it would create a vacuum so great as to pull everything in its path in on itself- it was surely her life. The black hole incarnate. She was thankful for the darkness, so that Karl wouldn't be staring at the people in the audience. It worked like a charm for him, too because he was able to focus on the stars and the lecture much better in the dark. Joni had read that a part of the schizophrenic's problem was over-stimulation of both sight and sound. She, herself, had trouble with glare and too much light. She preferred driving at night when there were fewer distractions. Were these signs of her own mild schizophrenia she wondered? Probably, but just thinking about these things taken to an extreme made it easier to imagine what Karl was experiencing.

After the show as they walked out, Karl put his arm around her tenderly. "Thank you," he said gently. "That was wonderful."

"I'm glad you liked it," she responded. "Did you get all of your questions answered?" Karl had said he would like to ask questions when they had discussed the possibility of going to the show a few days earlier.

"Most of them," he said. "But, did you see how out of proportion that planet was? If the mass of that planet was equal to ten suns, it wouldn't have been that small in relation to the other planets there...don't you think? Were you noticing that, too?"

"Uh, well, I guess..." Joni was amazed all over again. How in the world could someone so brilliant not understand that he needs help? Or was that it? Because he was brilliant, he thought he would know if he needed help - which is the whole problem. Uh oh, another mental Rubik's Cube...better leave that one alone.

On the way home they stopped for a light dinner and talked about what they had seen. Conversation was still sparse in comparison to normal folks, but Joni felt a new connection with the healthy part of Karl's brain. She wanted to encourage it to take over and save this person who was filled with so much promise.

When they arrived home Karl went to work on his writing. Joni did evening Gongyo and eventually went off to bed. Little more was said, but something of a bond had strengthened between them. They both slept well that night, but in the morning the sands beneath her progress had again shifted. Karl was distant and closed off as if in pain.

Joni was beginning to feel the strain of the months that were now stretching into three. A thought that hadn't crossed her mind in earlier days now visited frequently - what if this is going to be the way things are for the rest of my life? She decided to get busy and challenge the situation. Back on the daimoku campaign with vigor, she chanted to have a victory in the situation, whatever that might be. She was tired of being

180

wishy-washy and subject to reaction to her environment. She wanted to regain control of her life and to see clearly what steps she should take. The weather wasn't quite out of the winter rains as yet, but soon it would turn clear and warm again. She was starting to believe that she would have to send Karl packing once spring was firmly planted. Kevin would be visiting for the summer, and Joni's life revolved around him when he was home. It was also possible that Kevin would make the decision to move out permanently this year, now that he was getting old enough to decide. Joni didn't want to jeopardize that possibility by having a crazy homeless guy there indefinitely.

True, Kevin had been patient during the Christmas vacation, but he made no bones about the fact that he expected Karl to be gone for his upcoming Easter visit.

So Joni chanted. And then she chanted some more. She chanted for her son's happy life and for his understanding. She chanted to do the right thing and prayed desperately for wisdom. She chanted for Karl's happiness and for the best possible outcome for him and his family. But most of all, she determined to win in all areas of her life. She summoned up conviction and purpose and the will to do whatever she felt driven to do. 'Courage" was the Japanese calligraphy that hung on her wall - over and over she would look up at it as she chanted. Courage was what she needed most - and what she felt her leader, President Ikeda, had sent to her through this inscription.

Courage was the word she most needed to live by.

"Usually when people are sad, they don't do anything. They just cry over their condition. But when they get angry, they bring about a change."

— Malcolm X

Chapter Nine - Angry

Karl was angry now -all the time - beneath the surface. He would be civil and at times even force politeness, but his overall disgust with other people was paramount. Joni didn't take it too personally, although it was hard not to. She was, after all, a woman…which automatically qualified her for the worst of Karl's disdain.

Joni, in her weaker moments more frequently now, began to match energy with him.

Her own anger popped up in places where her diligence grew thin. She was now scurrying about for evidence whenever Karl was out of sight.

Did he drink his coffee laced with herbs - or did he just pour it down the drain? Had he taken a shower during the day when she wasn't home - indicating he had secretly returned home inappropriately? Were his clothes still in his dresser drawers? Were the cards he had given her still in the drawer of her altar table? And, now, added to the list - were there any knives missing?

You've got to be nuts yourself to keep him here if you're counting the knives now…she scolded herself. The cards filled with loving words from Christmas and Valentine's Day had disappeared and he later admitted to destroying them. Clothes would suddenly appear or disappear. She never knew now what he was smuggling home in his backpack. Then, there were the furtive trips to the bedroom every time she did gongyo. She could tell from the sounds she heard despite her chanting that he was stealing change - but what else was happening?

While he was in the shower she opened up his dresser drawer and found almost all of his clothes gone. "What did you do with your clothes, Karl?" she asked, trying to control her exasperation that bordered on anger.

"You're observant, "he said dryly.

"You hid them somewhere, Karl? Why did you do that?" Joni was clearly frustrated- which naturally put Karl off. Silence ensued for five minutes. Joni waited it out.

Finally Karl answered, "I don't know."

"Do you have another place to stay?" Joni insisted. But Karl had said all he was going to say.

Time was on his side and running out quickly for Joni. She needed to get to work. She'd have to figure this one out later. She only hoped that if he did have other plans, that he would let her in on them, so that she could put his parents' minds at ease.

All day at work she caught herself deep in thought with wrinkled brow. Was there a way of getting him to help - was he going to run away again? She found her detective nature taking over her thoughts and ultimately her actions. After work she

184

returned home and walked the property looking for his clothes. She knew where he had hidden his shoes when she wouldn't allow them into the house. The pine tree's base was naked save for pine needles. Where would he hide stuff? She tried to imagine his thoughts, his actions. But nothing gelled. She was glad that once again she had plans for the evening. She was receiving guidance from a senior leader, Mrs. McMullen.

She had planned on asking other questions, but the situation with Karl was now at near crisis magnitude. She felt in her bones that he wasn't coming home that night, but kept a sense of 'you-could-be-wrong' alive underneath her waves of conversation with the Japanese woman.

Joni loved Mrs. McMullen. She was round faced and pretty, in her sixties now, but always smiling a smile that escalated easily to a laugh. Similar in visage and demeanor to her grandmother who had passed on in recent years, she nurtured a part of Joni by her mere presence. Her husband had died in recent months - which Joni was shocked to learn. This was Mrs. M's third and best husband. That fact had always been a comfort to Joni - knowing that there was hope for a good relationship after divorce. Now she looked upon this ever-smiling woman with even more respect and admiration. *This little tiny aged woman drove for over an hour to come and give me guidance, when she is going through tremendous grief right now.* Joni was so amazed. What would most women her age, newly widowed be doing? Certainly not driving distances at night to help some half-baked Buddhist get a grip! Joni knew she had a long way to go to emulate this kind of character.

"If he doesn't come back, don't look for him," she was talking seriously now. Mrs.

McMullen was giving strict guidance – the kind that is down to earth and pulls no punches. "There are many people like that in the world…nice people, but they don't get well. It's their karma. You can't change that. There are hundreds of people like that in the world. You were able to help him chant 'Nam Myoho Renge Kyo' - so that's all you can do for him." She was referring to the fact that Karl had been exposed to Joni's Buddhist practice. Her broken English and Japanese heritage softened her words, but her eyes were definite.

Joni was agreeing, but also hoping that he would walk through the door. She wanted Mrs. McMullen to meet him for some reason. No such luck. The time passed quickly as they talked and soon it was time for Mrs. McMullen to leave on her long drive back to her own empty house. Joni didn't start dinner. She knew on some level that Karl wasn't going to show. Was he gone for good? She couldn't quite get a bead on that one - but her gut leaned more toward 'it ain't over yet' than 'the guy is history.' One thing she did feel sure of - he was okay - he was safe, and he was definitely not pulling on her psychic heart strings to rescue him.

She left the light on, just in case, and went to bed. Morning came without incident.

The light still burning brightly as a welcome home, but no one had come home. Joni felt centered and calm. It was going to be okay. She had done her part. She was not going to go and look for him again. As she sat down in front of her altar to do her morning prayers, she looked up to where a picture of Karl had been for two months. Empty. Her heart stopped. She whirled around on her still bent knees and looked to the mantel piece. The kissing picture and the picture of the two of them side by side were gone. *Wasn't that there last night?* She thought frantically to herself. *I'm sure it was!* But then her mind retraced the evening. She pictured again the conversation with Mrs. Mc Mullen and there it was - like a stop-frame action shot on her memory film. She was looking at Mrs. McMullen, engrossed in her conversation, but noticing a vacancy in the background that never registered until now. The

186

pictures <u>were</u> gone the night before, but she hadn't quite noticed.

She was crying in full sobs now. It hit her hard. Harder than it should, she thought, but there was no denying her pain. Then the pain gave way to curiosity and anger as she jumped up and ran into the bedroom. Sure enough! He had gone through the picture album she had put together of their adventures. Days on the beach, bittersweet and heavy with the harsh pronouncements of the judge still lingering in their ears. And happier times, when, he had insisted that they get a picture of the two of them kissing. Barbara had come through like a champ on that one. Then, she'd taken a few more of the two of them - Karl in his cowboy hat and all. Gone. The photos of the two of them were gone. As instinct took over now, Joni searched the pile of un-filed stuff that always mushroomed on her nightstand. She found the red and yellow envelope. Unbelievable! He had taken the negatives, too! Joni was on fire now. What right did he have to destroy those? They were her property, not his. A part of her felt scared inside, too. Would he want to eliminate *her* as well? She would be the only sad reminder of this time when he was weakest. He fell in love a bit - and he knew that she knew it. It was an embarrassment to him now. His shame was all consuming. Did this translate into something dangerous for her?

Joni felt a shift inside of her. Nothing would ever feel quite the same after today.

The age of innocence had reached its point of no return. She would sleep with one eye open for quite some time. It was clear - a resolution to this matter <u>had</u> to come swiftly. She had no choice but to see it through - even if that meant hearing about what happened to him some time in the future - she knew she would eventually have closure. She pulled herself together and went off to work. Work was such a treasure at times like this. The gift of having a job to go to was more valuable than all the gold on earth during these days.

Karl never did come home that night. But the next day at work, Joni got the call that now was almost predictable. Karl would take the bus to Sebastopol - they could talk tonight. Fine. She wasn't happy, she wasn't sad; she was confused - yet clear. She had to set him straight on what was and what wasn't acceptable behavior. Staying out all night without calling was definitely unacceptable. Stealing was unacceptable. In the middle of her tirade she noticed Karl was taking it all in stride.

"I can promise you that I won't ever do that again," he said with that truthful straight- on sparkling eyes look. He must have scared himself, she thought.

One thing about him - he was able to keep his word - especially when he looked her right in the eye. Never boring - that was the best description of his life as it intertwined with hers.

Joni's letter of 3-7-94 read:

Dear Elaine & Donald:

Just a quick update. Karl came home Fri. nite. I told him it was not okay to stay out all night without calling, etc. and that the pictures he took (he did destroy them and the negatives) were not his to take. I told him that I knew something had happened to him as a child and that I was sorry he had been hurt. He said, "You could help...I still owe the $75...you could help me pay it." I said, "That is a product of your stealing...not of your having been hurt" - this annoyed him - he packed up and left - but came back in ½ hour. He was hungry.

So - he stayed - but I'm feeling less and less tolerant - which I'm sure he will pick up on. For instance, we went to the movies

188

yesterday and on the way out - as usual, he got ahead of me and let the door go in my face. I asked him on the way to the car why he always did that - did he feel superior by doing it? He, of course, had no comment.

Earlier - we had gone to the flea market - I went to hold his arm and he jerked it away. Then, as is his usual style, he took off in another direction and we spent our time there alone. I came very close to leaving him there when I couldn't locate him, but finally made an announcement over the PA and he showed up. He said he had been looking for me - which may have been true.

Anyway, this type of treatment has been largely overlooked the past three weeks. He has always acted this way, but there used to be kinder compensations - and real affection to offset it - now it's harder to take. I'm trying to formulate a plan of action in my head - I feel badly that I can't help Karl to choose a healthier course of action, but it really is his choice at this point. His writings still show confusion and the constant categorization of good and evil. Maybe his legacy is to turn all feelings of love into hate - if he rejects and belittles us long enough he gets to be right...we do stop caring - or at least we run for cover.

Still - it's not over yet - I'll keep him warm and fed until he chooses to move on.

Love, Joni

Joni was stunned - Karl was *again* asking for her to pay his fine. With her obvious anger at the thought - he withdrew in his own anger. She suddenly became clear that he was a mirror for her. "Thank you for showing me how self-centered I have been," she said genuinely. Then she apologized for any pain that she had caused him in this life or past ones. She realized that she tied herself to him with negative energy, and had to release it in order to be free. She was also tied to him with

189

positive energy, and that part she could use to respect his life as best she could.

She also felt that his parents needed to see him. She had to be a mirror for them.Had they ever really known their son? Their real son, or had they seen him through the lens of his accomplishments, and his failures? Did they see the person inside that needed them, still? Or was their own troubled relationship more than they could deal with at just the moment when he needed them? Joni felt the shifting sand beneath her feet. She needed them to understand Karl, to accept him, to stop being afraid.

"I have a son, who is a... not an ordinary form of schizophrenia, but clearly, cannot take care of himself. And the great fear of then, of all parents is, when the parents die, who takes care of your child? And the answer is: they become homeless."

-James D. Watson

Chapter Ten   Hair-brained

Karl had gone to the library for the day and Joni thought she'd surprise him and give him a ride home. Most days now when she'd go in to pick him up he would be at one of the tables or a chair at the end of the bookshelf usually with a book open. There were times when he would just be staring into space...waiting for her to come and break the trance. Sometimes he would report on how much he had written and would be eager to continue his work after dinner at home. Other times he said little and Joni surmised that he had accomplished little. It was a strange phenomenon to observe. He had been really excited at one point because he had spent time writing in a local café and the owner had somewhat befriended him. But, it was just a matter of time before he was caught stealing his coffee refills and, too, the owner began to notice that he was abnormal. So he had been asked to leave and not come back. Hence, the library had become a refuge. It lacked the excitement and energy of a restaurant with all of its sounds, sights and smells. Everyone was quiet and subdued - and this was not conducive to keeping the sleep-deprived stimulated.

191

Joni marveled that he wasn't fast asleep each time she found him.

This day was different, though. Karl wasn't in the library at the appointed time. He had always been where he'd said he'd be when he'd said he'd be there, so Joni felt it a bit odd. The day was sunny and warm, so she guessed that he may have gone for a walk, or perhaps even decided to walk home early. She placed herself in his shoes once again trying to hone in on the route he might have taken. After a brief pause she got into the car and began her homeward search. He was nowhere to be seen as she came upon the last mile before home. Luckily, at a stop sign, she was able to look down a side street and see him walking toward her. He seemed somewhat startled to s e e her, but quickly changed his demeanor as if he had been waiting for her to show up.

"What's going on?" Joni asked as he got into the car. "You weren't at the library - I just thought I might find you walking home..." she chided playfully.

Karl did not answer. He was heavy with thought...no, more than that, he was scared. Joni scrambled mentally to understand what was going on with him. She sensed he was wrestling with something deep inside and that she had just become a kind of mental flotation device for him to cling to in the waves. "Were you walking long?" She asked gingerly and then followed his silence with, "Are you all right, Karl?"

Karl shook his head yes, but his eyes were riveted out the windshield and vacant to the sights beyond. Joni felt his pain and his struggle. She could only guess that the Terrors were back, but in a newer, more virulent strain. She felt certain that some memories had been triggered and long suppressed knowledge was making its way to the surface. This was dangerous without professional help, but there was no way to control what seemed to be happening.

Once in the door Karl immediately got out his paints and a fresh piece of paper.

Normally he liked to paint during the night while Joni was sleeping, but tonight he was working as if someone very big and bad was chasing him. Joni left him alone while she made dinner. She was hoping that her thoughts would not interrupt his process…yet she wanted to stay alert and available should he want to talk. She moved more quietly than usual in the tiny kitchen, placing pots and pans gently on the stove, being careful not to rattle the silverware.

She called him for dinner and they sat down quietly to eat. "Do you want to talk about what happened today?" She asked slowly and quietly. Karl shook his head. She felt in his gesture not so much a refusal as an inability to speak.

His eyes seemed to be searching the innards of his brain to find the words that would express what he'd been through. The arrogance of other days, the seething anger just beneath the surface of his pleasantries was wholly absent. Joni knew that to pry verbally or physically was out of the question. She decided to just energetically send him love and compassion and tell him on a spiritual level that she was there for him. It seemed to work, and he slowly softened as if his fear was backing away carefully from a cliff. He thanked her sincerely for the dinner and then retired to finish his work.

When Joni was halfway through washing the dinner dishes, he popped in to the kitchen with his still-wet painting to show her. Joni's eyes flew open as she took a look. Karl's other paintings had all been dark. They had black backgrounds and a definitely midnight feel to them - not really something she would have wanted to hang up. They were primitive and flat dimensionally - and seemed almost preachy in their presentation. But this was completely different. Red, orange

193

and yellow filled the page in vibrant, violent shocks from a tortured human face in the center. If there was ever an expression of a face in Hell - this was it.

"That is <u>incredible</u>!" She immediately exclaimed. "Karl, I can't believe it! You have so much talent!" She was aware that she was gushing and in comparison to her reaction to his other paintings was feeling a bit sheepish about it, but hoped he wouldn't notice.

Karl grinned, "I call it 'Hairbrained'", he said "because see all of this hair..." He pointed to the flame-like tentacles emanating not only from the top of the head, but the entire face.

"I love it!" Joni wasn't going to let up now... not until he'd had enough. "Karl, you might be able to become an artist and sell you work for a living." She was hoping this would sound encouraging and not capitalistic - but she was aware that it was a loaded statement. Karl nodded his head vigorously - not wanting to spoil the fun of the moment. Then he announced that he was going to go out for a walk. This was now a routine consequence of having felt close to Joni for even moments at a time. She understood immediately and bade him a nice walk. She was somewhat pleased, herself, to be left alone with the painting, so that she could really study it.

The passion that was obvious here was as though some internal dam had broken.

Joni could only look in awe and feel deeply encouraged. She would in future days make color photocopies of all of his works - just in case he later regretted them and felt compelled to destroy them. She wondered how he would feel - years from now, looking at the face of his torment. Would he have self-compassion and be proud of his progress or would he shrink from these titanic days? Her heart wanted to preserve him for himself. Was it sensible and respectful, as she felt - or merely an exercise in control? She was devoid of judgment.

A delicate balance tipped in Karl's favor. He was getting somewhere, Joni felt. The truth was, she was hoping this was the case. It was altogether possible that he was emotionally backing up against a wall. Joni knew that he would have to get through his anger to reach his pain in order to heal. Today she felt that this had happened in some measure. She watched an interesting program on PBS about children who kill.

Literally, child murderers. The program covered a couple and their breakthrough therapy which involved holding the child tightly in a hug until he or she was able to get past his anger and reach his pain. Joni knew that Karl was physically too large for this type of therapy, but psychically, she could envelope him with love until he felt safe enough to feel. Why? Why bother? Why was she tuned in to these therapies, these books, these articles? Who knew? She just was and it was her place at this time in her life. Of this she was certain.

What was less certain was how this would come to some kind of conclusion. On days like this, she felt progress was being made and was energized to see it through. On other days the whole thing seemed ludicrous at best and out of whack to say the least. It could be a fact of life that this scenario would stretch out for years into the future. Did she have that much compassion in her? Not really. But faced in her mind's eye with his dead corpse on a plane to Minneapolis, she kept putting one foot in front of the other.

Her reports to his parents were now tinged with weariness, now hopeful and light. But the variations were becoming closer ends of the same spectrum - and she had become bolder now with her observations. She no longer cared how nutty her theories sounded. In fact, on this day in March her letter was accompanied by what she had found when she read the bumps on Karl's still shaven head! The pages of her book were highlighted in colors corresponding to the diagram of sections of the skull where Karl's bumps were most prominent.

1. A large bump in this area indicated so great an interest in the opposite sex as to prove a handicap - unless sublimated, turning the person to religious or charitable works.

16. Indicates respect and perhaps veneration in the religious sense - too large pointed to a subservient nature and perhaps religious mania.

24. Observation - denoted ability to differentiate between one thing and another- ability to take in one's environment. Too large suggested the spy and the gossip.

32. Memory for events - showed good memory denoting a successful student. It was fascinating that these were the particular areas of prominence on Karl's head. Many of the other sections were unrelated to his personality - which was equally interesting to note. Donald and Elaine never really commented too much on the "research", but Joni was fully engaged by the coincidence.

Her letter of March 11 otherwise read:

Dear Elaine and Donald:

Karl is gone again. Was not at our meeting place last night, but I do expect he'll call by the end of the day. You will probably know all of this before you get this letter.

I wanted to enclose copies of his paintings and some of his writings.

The section on women is rather sad, but I wanted you to see it…it's one section that I was able to sneak out to make copies. Most of the other stuff that he's had on his computer disk is about God and evolution, etc….but, hopefully, someday, we'll get to read through it. There were a few nicer poems that I was able to copy down that really touched me:

Joni

You must think that I'm some kind of bee
or maybe a gnat or a flea
When I tell the truth
You say, "You already tried Ruth!"
 And I must enter some kind of plea.

Sleep

Sleep is our selfish, lower nature asserting itself. Overcome sleep and you will free yourself from future sins.
Sleep is like a cloud which comes from behind and envelopes us with sweet whisperings
Again, sleep is a block of ice which falls
on our head when we are not looking.

It is the only enemy and must be destroyed utterly.

Love and Heartaches

Love doesn't love without an ache,
The heart and head of the lover to break.
For to be lovable we must grow
To grow, there must be change
there must be some pain.

True Love

Don't talk about love, lover!

Slap my face!

A true lover never talks about love,

Because if he could have done something more, He would have done it.
If he could have thought something more, He would have thought it.
He has already done all his powers will allow. They fail, and therefore it is finished.
He hopes it is beautiful.

Karl told me the other night that God told him that he was smarter than all of his professors and that was why they couldn't understand him. He specifically mentioned a paper he did on Jesus at St. John's College where he extrapolated some theory on His second coming. He got an 'F'. I asked him how long ago this happened… he said 11 or 12 years ago. This points to me that Karl's thoughts have long been distorted and that a change toward what we would call a healthy outlook could actually mean death to him. (In his own mind)

What is the answer? I really don't know. I love Karl the way he is, but because of that I want for him to be able to connect with the world, to be seen as the kind and brilliant man that he is. This would involve changing him. I want to comfort him through this painful process, but he sees my comfort as a deception and a fraud. He tries me (as he has many others) to the point of proving his stubborn truth…that he is bad and unworthy of love…but he wouldn't know love if he was completely submerged in it. I can only pray along with the hundreds of others who are doing this…for his true happiness, whatever form that takes. If being right is more important to him than anything else in life, he will never choose to alter his perceptions. This is something we must face.

I asked him the other morning if he would ever go back to teaching. He said it wasn't for him to decide. I told him that it was and that if he didn't make active decisions about his life that other people would make decisions for him. He said he thought God knew what He was doing. I said God does, but you still need to take control of your own life...will go into more detail when we talk. It comes down to whether or not he will accept responsibility for his own life. Right now it doesn't look positive, but as long as he's alive there's hope...

Love,
Joni

Karl's lengthy section of writings on Women followed. It was very discouraging in part - especially to Karl's mom, but Joni felt it was important that they understand as many facets of Karl as was possible.

WOMEN

TO YH

Say, look here, I've had enough.

I know you're tender and sweet, and not rough. Let's leave this mess, this awful cancer.
I'll just be your timorous dancer.
Is there an answer besides rotten oblivion? YH, just keep me away from that woman!
Worship MOM and be blissful, it's true, it's true.

Jam your head through the pavement, it's good for you, too.

NO BUTS ABOUT IT

Father was sweeter, but Mom was a cheater.

JONI

"I was looking for God; he asked you me to shelter. You ignored me, and left us helter-skelter."
* If I had a wife
Who didn't want my life I'd fiddle in my prime, Work all day for a dime,
And minding my manners, too.

Right now, though, It's a different show.

If I had a thousand eyes,
And the first was the key to the other 999, I'd not look at you.
See my brain's kind of sensitive. I'm not saying this tentative.
I'd rather be drowned 10 times than smile when you smile.
I smile at things God-begot. You smile at, I know not what.

WHAT YOU'VE BEEN MISSING

If to the women you carefully listen,
You'll see all the things you've been missing.

You'll see how they carefully blend in with your style, however they may feel themselves, while it serves their guile.

You'll see how they contradict you left and right, and contradict themselves, to complete your plight!
You'll see how not following their well thought-out advice will lead you not to hell or death, but something worse.

Of course, of thinking they may never be accused
We think for both them and us—and then we lose.

You'll see how they like to incite your anger,
when you, all innocent, have kept them from danger.

You'll see how they blame you for everything under the sun,
Though your neck is sweating, and not one lick of work have they done.

The desire to see women is a true curse;

It drags you straight down, makes you ready for the hearse.
If the nation would be strong,
Men must learn to stand alone.

Parts of Karl's writings brought up feelings of anger and disgust; parts compassion and empathy. The reality was that she could feel his intense hatred of women, which was almost equally matched with his intense attraction to them. As was her custom, at least in her more enlightened moments, Joni began to search her own life for the causes she had made to bring this situation into her life. After chanting and opening up to her own innate darkness, she realized how she had become a man-basher. Her words like, "What do you expect from a man? Or, that's a man for you..." had become far too lightly tripping off her tongue.

An expanded view unfolded before her as she chanted. She realized that there were many men she deeply loved, her father, her brothers, grandparents, friends and she realized that to bash 'men' in general meant to bash even those she loved. True, she had been hurt by men several times - but her cause was suddenly clear to her - which meant that she was now free to change it. She vowed to cease and desist immediately. She would pay closer attention to the words she said about men and generalizations of any kind. This wasn't the decision of a goody-two-shoes; this was the decision of a woman who wanted very much to eliminate a source of her own suffering. It was also a decision that ultimately brought her back in line with her true self - a woman who loved many people, both male and female.

With that new determination an interesting phenomenon came about. Karl's piercing words no longer cut her as she read them. She was able to naturally detach the message from the messenger. She was able to view his life and suffering with compassion, regardless of the fact that much of his anger was in the written sense, directed right at her. It was a freeing, maturing feeling that would serve her in good stead for many years to come.

Still she had to laugh to herself. Don't most people get this lesson with a lot less trauma and confusion? Joni, she said to herself, you always have to make it difficult, don't you? Colorful…that's what they'll say about you…if you have any friends left to say anything after all of this! Normal was certainly not going to be a word that swam about her in torrents. But, then, who is normal?

"When you are inspired by some great purpose, some extraordinary project, all your thoughts break their bounds. Your mind transcends limitations, your consciousness expands in every direction and you find yourself in a new, great and wonderful world. Dormant forces, faculties and talents become alive, and you discover yourself to be a greater person by far than you ever dreamed yourself to be."

- Patanjali

Chapter Eleven   Irony

Joni read the newspaper clippings sent to her from Karl's father. Irony was heavy…accolades from his staff and students…awards and yet…his own son so lost to him.

"John Jackson Named Minnesota College Professor of the Year". The article spoke of how 400 candidates for the honor had been nominated, but it was Dr. Jackson who had won the prestigious award. Past and present students described him as a mentor, instilling confidence and unleashing potential, as being a person who changed their lives. "Dr. Jackson introduced us to plant after plant as though they were his old friends and I discovered that I, too, had a passion for plants," said Jane E., doctoral student in the Plant Biological Sciences program at the University of Minnesota. "I often wonder what I would be doing today if Dr. Jackson had not inspired me the way he did. I've come to believe that he knew or saw something of which I was not yet fully aware."

The article went on to praise Jackson for his efforts in obtaining a scanning electron microscope (SEM) for the college and mentioned his discoveries of new plants in Mexico and Central America. He was internationally known for these discoveries. As Joni read, she felt a sense of loss and sadness. Here was this father trying to impress his son on the one hand and feeling totally inadequate on the other. Was this part of the problem? Had he taught his son to be bigger than life - and been unable to hide his disappointment in the result? Joni felt that he would sincerely be thrilled for Karl's accomplishments, too - but maybe Karl sensed that it would be for the wrong reasons. His son was perhaps mainly an extension of himself...and was to be successful at the very least. But, maybe Karl had other plans...or maybe living up to his father's reputation had proven too burdensome. Whatever the cause, this first-born son was definitely out of orbit with the original parental plan.

Still, Dr. Jackson's accomplishments were nothing to be sneezed at. His example of self-actualization could have gone either way...it could have been a major source of encouragement to Karl as well. Joni was sure that she would probably never know all of the nuances of what Karl's life had been and how or if environment had played a role in his illness. She was sure of one thing, though, and that was that the whole family needed help. Not unlike most families, the need for help and understanding would not generate the impetus of its own to seek that help. This, too, was all right - because there was simply no other way to look at it and accept it. So, life as usual would resume at some not-too-distant point regardless of Karl and his condition.

In this case as well as in most others she knew of, families thrived on a certain level of dysfunction. This became crystal clear to her as the months unfolded. If too much were to change too drastically in too short a span of time, the family could disintegrate. So much of how we relate to other family members is based on past information or stereotypes we have devised ourselves. This was a reality check for her.

She knew that once again she would have to step back and be an impartial observer- even though her emotions could take her back and forth endlessly between feelings. Was it her place to interfere with whatever Karl's family had created? Had she been drawn in to it all or was she allowing herself to be? What of her own family? Would her own parents, to whom's house her apartment was attached, decide they needed Karl to be gone? What of their safety? Was she imperiling them in anyway?

Was she, in fact, testing the limits of her own family's patience to a point from which she could not recover? Her parents had not interfered at all, but she knew if her father gave her an ultimatum, there would be no arguing. Despite the fact that she paid rent, it was, after all still his house.

Her focus sharpened and she once again renewed her determination to see the project before her to completion. Completion…what form would it take?

Joni received some background information from Elaine and Karl that took the wind out of her sails. It was important to her to read these letters, but it also saddened her. The problem seemed to reach deeper back and further down than she had envisioned. But she read the letters over several times in hopes of gleaning some answer or at least a direction for future action.

On St. John's College letterhead was a letter from Karl's Professor and roommate to Elaine and Donald. It was dated August 2, 1983.

Dear Dr. and Mrs. Jackson,

It is not easy for me to answer your letter. I want to begin by saying that I think very highly of Karl as a person and as a student at St. John's. He has a fine character, an excellent upbringing and a very good mind.

I have no more understanding of what took place in his thinking than you have acquired already and express in your letter. I indeed was concerned, as you are, by the enormous energy that he devoted to his 'meditation.' I too feel that the influence of Eknath Easwaran is much too great on him. His thinking about it seems to me to be much too uncritical. Like many young men his age, he is intensely self-critical and inclined to be self-absorbed, while at the same time being highly idealistic. I cannot agree with much in Easwaran's thinking. I deeply disapprove of any teacher taking over a disciple body and soul as he seems prepared to do in Karl's case. This may be more Karl's doing than his, but the effect seemed to me altogether unfortunate.

On the other hand, Karl has visited there for long enough to know that he was happy and perhaps more outgoing with these people, with whom he felt he shared important 'spiritual' goals, than he was here. Sometime after his return from the spring vacation I felt I had to speak rather sharply to him about his almost morose presence as a guest in my house. It is my sense that he is naturally friendly and could easily become more involved with other people if it were not for his 'meditation' and what underlies it. As it is, he withdrew increasingly all year. After I spoke to him he made real efforts to mitigate some aspects of his behaviour that were simply becoming oppressive to me. He is a very nice, kind and thoughtful person, but his dedication to this way of being can make him most difficult to be with closely. I am glad to hear you are finding him more relaxed. I am sure he has no intention to offend or to hurt.

He was always considerate to me and cooperated in the somewhat stringent requirements I imposed about our sharing

206

the kitchen together. We did a few things together routinely and he seemed to enjoy them at least on the surface. He enjoyed being helpful on occasion, although his first priority was always the immense amounts of time he spent 'meditating'. It was not in my view good for him at all.

I wish I could help you understand the situation in any way. As far as his studies go, he was learning a great deal here. It is quite correct that St. John's education is not strictly pre-medical and therefore leaves a good deal for the student to do on his own before he can reasonably expect to be admitted to medical school. Many of our students go on to study medicine, but most of them have to spend a year making up for those omissions. While I think this swayed Karl somewhat in his decision to leave St. John's, I am quite sure that the pull toward Petaluma was the original and dominating force.

I believe that Karl will insist on going along this road as far as he can. I hope he will either come to see its limitations, or else to discover in it more that will bring out what is fine and appealing in him, what is generous rather than what turns him in on himself. For the most part at this time I believe it cuts him off from others and from the wonderful things in the world around him. I fear that he is learning to hide his true thoughts and feelings, just because they do separate him in a radical way from human affection. That he denies this is at least a good sign. I found him unprepared to examine or discuss these ideas seriously. It is as though he were needing to be told what to think. Yet he is an independent character and thinker when he chooses to be.

Several of his teachers felt that he had grown not only as a student with respect to his studies, but in his role in the classes, which are conducted here very largely through conversation. He seemed to be easier and friendlier, less prone to harsh criticism and sullen silence. When he was not entirely withdrawn into himself I enjoyed his company. We shared several meals a week and maintained on the surface pleasant relations, though I felt I could not even guess what he was really thinking or feeling. He does not share those things easily and I did not succeed in bringing him out. Certainly his religion, by its very nature, takes the meaning out of 'merely' human feelings.

Nonetheless, after a great deal of though and hesitation, I told him he might return to live here next year if he wished to. I hoped that that offer might encourage him to consider returning to St. John's where he has learned a lot, above all how to learn even more. St. John's has done him a lot of good. However, I did not expect him to return, as he indicated that in all probability he would not. Your letter confirms what he already told me. I am sad about that, most of all for his sake, but also because I felt as I never felt before that we had remained largely strangers in spite of seeing each other several times each day.

I am sorry not to be helpful. I believe that nothing but patience and goodwill can help at all.

Sincerely yours,

Robert Zant.

Joni was crestfallen. The issues with Karl stretched further back than she had thought. This was a deeper quagmire than she first thought. She put the letter down and picked up the others that Donald and Elaine had also included; one from Karl to Easwaran and one from them to Karl:

August 1985

Dear Easwaran,

208

I wrote to the medical schools who had chosen me as an alternate and told them that I'd decided not to accept alternate status. This means that next year I will be joining you in Petaluma. I should be able to make enough money over the summer here to support myself for a while; so I could work at the ashram when I come in mid-August.

It turned out that my parents were not very upset over my decision - I mean, they were upset, but I went for a mountain walk instead of letting them yell at me. In a few days when things were a little calmer, it turns out what they were really concerned about is that I should have a career of some kind, and we were agreed on that.

On June 15 I'll be graduating from the U of M with a degree in philosophy. I'd invite you to come to the ceremonies, but you must be busy with your duties at the ashram, and after all you do live a considerable distance from here. The possibilities now are kind of confusing; I could go to graduate school in philosophy and become a philosophy professor; or reapply to medical school; or work in some other medically related field or non-medically related field. I would like to talk to you to see how I could best serve you and the ashram.

With love, Karl

P.S. We saw a movie the other day about Mozart's life called "Amadeus." It portrayed Mozart as a somewhat muddle-headed person who was driven to death from self- condemnation because he didn't go to be with his father. I can't believe Mozart wasn't more one-pointed than that. I mean, he was always drinking and dividing his attention, and seemed totally unable to control his passions. It just doesn't seem like he could have produced any meaningful work from such a state of mind.

2 December 1992

Dearest Son:

We were glad to talk to you on Tuesday. We have enclosed the check for $250 you asked for. Please watch your spending judiciously in order to get yourself to your first pay check.

You have promised us that you will see a psychiatrist. We also feel that you need to be completely honest with the psychiatrist and describe your activities since leaving home. We feel you owe yourself and your parents that. It is not too much to ask.

Since your birthday we have sent you nearly $1,000. You now have another opportunity to provide for yourself. You seemed to feel you had the job in the nursing home.

Before you begin work at the nursing home, you have time to learn how to request both general assistance aid and general medical assistance aid. You should be ready in case you find yourself without money again. All you have to do is find (probably county) office and ask questions. This could be done on the telephone with you taking notes.

Remember that you are always welcome here and we are willing to pay for an airline ticket to home the next time you fall into hard times. I have inquired as to how you can receive general assistance and general medical assistance here. You are eligible in Minnesota after spending only one night here.

The matter of the money going to Todd needs to be addressed. You need to tell Todd that when you gave him that money it set off a series of events that became very expensive to your family. (Karl gave Todd $100 - This put him on the street) That money needs to come back to the family as soon as possible. This amounts to our supporting Todd and you - that is not proper in any sense.

210

Karl, we did reach Todd this morning. He said he did not know that taking your money put you on the street homeless and broke. We informed Todd that the money actually was now owed to us and that he must pay it back as soon as possible. He does not have a job. He said that we needed to straighten you out about God. A true friend would not use you to extract a large sum of money from. He took advantage of you.

This must be made right. (Todd was a drug addict who told Karl that his mother would be evicted if he didn't get money. He took Karl's last $100 and spent it on drugs)

Mom and I are willing to do anything to help you Karl. Unfortunately, at this point it is not just financial help you actually need. We trust your promise that you will seek continual psychiatric help and that you will be kind enough to contact us once a week to honestly describe how you are.

We love you more than you can know. Please take good care of your body and your mind.

All Our Love, God Bless You,

Mom and Dad

As Joni read these letters over she saw the span of time unfold before her eyes…the problem was well over ten years in the making…and Karl had promised to seek psychiatric help that he never followed through on. What was to make her think that he would now? If anything, he probably felt less in need now than he did then.

She was growing impatient with Karl and his attitude. He seemed to be a guest only in the house, but Joni had come to see him as a card-carrying roommate. She resented the fact that he never washed a dish; only helped with the cooking on rare occasions; and had not done much at all in the way of housework. She was lamenting this fact to Elaine over the phone one Saturday - feeling embarrassed at the same time. She was tattling to his mom that he hadn't done his fair share - *reduced to this*, she thought, but she couldn't hold back. Elaine came through for her as she often did these days. "Go find him and tell him you need help," she said. "You just make him come home. He'd probably want to anyway. Don't be afraid to ask for what you need."

"That makes sense," Joni felt dumber than usual. *Of course,* she thought, *I do have a right to ask for help. What's the worst that can happen?* "Thanks, Elaine, - I'm going to do it," she said with determination in her voice. "The worst he can do is say no..."

"Exactly," Elaine encouraged.

Joni was overcoming her embarrassment now and opened up to Elaine. "I guess I've always been afraid to ask for help. It's always just been easier to do things for myself." She was realizing in a moment of epiphany that this was one of the major lessons Karl was teaching her. She, too had a right to ask for help.

"Let me know what happens," said Elaine as they said good-bye.
"I will," Joni replied, "I'll write."

After she hung up the receiver she got on her shoes and did sansho as she left the house. Sansho meant to chant 'Nam Myoho Renge Kyo' three times and was a form of respect. As she got into her car she chanted for the courage to confront Karl. It was a deeply rude awakening for her to realize that she felt real terror with the idea of asking for help. Wow! She thought, what the heck have I been doing all of these years? Time to grow up for sure! Simultaneously she was half-hoping that he wouldn't be at the library as he said. If she couldn't find him, she couldn't confront him after all.

As she parked the car she took a deep breath and continued to chant softly to herself. She got out of the car with confidence. Her steps felt sure and heavy, but there was no anger attached to her stride. She entered the small library and sure enough, there sat Karl. She walked up to him and gently said, "Hi. I was wondering if you would be available to help me around the house a bit?"

Karl looked up and nodded yes as he jumped to his feet and started packing up his back-pack. "You don't have to come right this minute," Joni hesitated…"I've got to go to the store and I could pick you up on the way back if you prefer…"

"No, that's fine," Karl was docile and agreeable. "I'm not getting much work done here, anyway."

"Great!" Joni answered and they left together.

When Joni wrote to Elaine on March 22nd her letter said:

Dear Donald & Elaine:

Thanks for the letters and the check! Also, thanks so much for your extra time and support over the phone.

Elaine, you were right…I went to find Karl at the library on Saturday and told him I needed help. He was happy to help me! He did all the vacuuming and swept and mopped the kitchen floor. On Sunday he had planned to go out in the morning, but stayed home instead. He helped prepare a vegetable tray for my mother's birthday party and voluntarily swept up the mess he made! He really seemed happy most of the weekend.

213

He came to the family gathering for my mother and seemed to enjoy himself, but after a while went back over to my apartment to write. It was very easy and comfortable. No one was concerned or offended. Everyone tends to mill about and drift off here and there in our family anyway.

He's been letting me hug him, but still no kissing, holding hands or hugging back. He did tease me yesterday morning calling me a witch and I grabbed him and threatened to beat him up all in good fun...he seemed to like the attention and the touching.

I gave him his mail from you, Elaine, last night. He opened it, but didn't say anything. I was in the kitchen and asked what you had sent...was it an Easter card? He said, "Yes" and dropped the subject. This morning he was noticeably depressed again. I asked if hearing from his mother upset him and he said, "No". He slept well last night; this may still be a source of discouragement to him.

My son, Kevin, talked to me a great deal on Sunday. He is thinking seriously about moving back in with me. Karl heard the whole conversation from my end as he was in the living room. I later asked him how he felt about the idea and he said it was fine with him and that he liked Kevin. I mentioned that Kevin does have a foul mouth, which was Karl's only objection to him in December. Karl didn't say anything more. Quite honestly, Kevin would prefer that Karl not be here. I've told him that I do respect his thoughts and feelings, but that I will still do what I think I must do. (I expect him to live this way, too - to be as true to himself as possible) Kevin will be out in April for a short visit and perhaps will see a change for the better in Karl. If things do not go well then, we'll have to work out the wrinkles as best we can. I think that Karl can be a help to Kevin and that Kevin can be a help to Karl as well...but it will be up to the two of them to make those decisions. After I spoke with Kevin I

214

said to Karl, "You must really think I'm a really strange mother the way I speak to my son." (Because I really talk to Kevin as if he's an adult in many ways) Karl said, "Parts of it (my parenting style) are really bizarre…but, bizarre on the surface and very profound underneath." I felt complimented and thanked him. I told him that I usually don't care what people think of my behavior, but that I do care what he thinks.

After reading Dr. Zant's letter I feel several things…sad that Karl has such an extremely long history of denying his feelings and on the other hand, encouraged that he has been able to express his feelings of love for me…whether real or not. The hard part in my way of seeing things is that as Prof. Zant alludes, there is something underlying this choice Karl has made to be "esoteric". This, I feel, is what we are really up against because without his desire to feel differently, there can basically be no help. Even if we were able to forcibly get lithium into him, I don't feel it would change his basic belief system which is hell-bent on controlling himself. He is incredibly strong in this regard.

I would like to see him get any help possible, but I also know that in some way he must consent to it. This is not out of the question by any means.

If we can look at this from a Buddhist perspective for just a moment, I'll explain what I'm doing.

In terms of my own life (which is the only thing I can change) my suffering around or because of Karl's illness is my karma.

Because everything in our environment is a reflection of our own lives (Buddhist concept of Esho Funi) there is something in my life that has attracted this painful/joyful situation.

I can choose to really change my karma by focusing on my own happiness and what I really need/want for a victory in my own life.

Through my Buddhist practice I am determined to show actual proof of the validity of this philosophy and create a victorious life for myself and my family...this means changing me, not Karl.

Because of this and because of Karl, and your support and guidance, I've been able to really see myself. It was so difficult for me to ask him for help...I would rather stick a hot poker in my eye than ask for help...I think Karl feels this way, too. I am continuing to challenge myself to be vulnerable with him whether or not he rejects me. This, I feel, is the only way to really instruct him, by showing him how it's done. I know I have a ways to go, but I have really learned a lot through all of this, and I think that Karl is learning at lightning speed, too. I think that's why he's still here. I do need prodding to take the next step each time, as I did on Saturday. It's scary for me to change, just like it is for everyone else...but I'm determined to have a happy life with or without Karl...so I must change.

In the meantime, I am still doing my best to enjoy each day...not making that dependent on anyone or anything else. If we can only be happy when there are external circumstances that please us, we are in trouble...because there will always be problems in life.

Please know that in helping me, you are helping Karl immeasurably. He is so observant and keen, he watches everything I do and on some level he wants to join me in laughing at life!

Love, Joni

She hoped they would see their son from a new perspective. Perhaps because she had separated from Kevin's father early on in Kevin's life, she knew that a child was not a possession. He was a full human being and could not ever belong to her alone. Yet, it was her duty to protect him with her life. This is how she thought most parents felt. But the control of a child had nebulous borders. Control to protect, yes. But, control to gain power over, that got tricky. So, as she watched the drama emerge before her of the life that led up to and would stretch beyond this point in time, she tried to imagine with compassion the dynamics of this family. Nothing about it felt easy. Nothing about it seemed wrong, either. It just felt as though there was no room for this illness in their lives.

Why should there be? Who would ever make room for illness in their life? But, it was here, and it was here to stay for a very long visit. How terrifying that must be for them, she thought

Her own worries didn't have much time to blossom. She needed to remain optimistic, but she knew that this kind of tragedy could strike any family at any time. She had to learn as much as possible from her experience. Although an ugly prospect, it could someday be a blessing to have learned this well.

"...a great human revolution in just a single individual will help achieve a change in the destiny of a nation, and further, will enable a change in the destiny of all mankind..."

– Daisaku Ikeda

Chapter Twelve   Wearing Down

Karl was gone again. Joni, now an old hand at the routine was fairly certain that he would return. It was just a matter of time. She had scolded him for keeping her awake at night as he went in and out for walks through the sliding glass door.

"Karl, I need to sleep. I have to work in the morning," she said sharply at about midnight. Karl had gone out for a walk and just returned through the double-sized sliding glass door. The whole framework shook as he opened it each time and it rumbled through the house. "My parents' room is right over there," she pointed. The noise of that door opening and closing will disturb them, too." The wraparound deck ran the length of the house with large sliding glass doors to several rooms. The vibrations of the doors opening and closing or footsteps on the deck were noticeable down the line of the house.

Karl said nothing. He was angry and trying to figure out what to do next. Joni went back to bed. An hour later she heard the door opening and closing over and over. Karl had gone out to the garage and found some 3-in-One oil and was oiling the door.

"This will make it quiet," he said scowling as she approached seething.

"No, Karl, it won't. Please put that back. It's the weight of this door that makes the noise…not the track. I insist that you either stay in or out." She stomped back to bed. *I am not going to lose any more sleep over this,* she said to herself as she got back under the covers. Getting into a huge control drama was going to sap her energy for the other parts of her life, so she refused to do it. She had stated her demand and knew that Karl would either abide or face the consequence of being thrown out for good.

He took off. Three hours later he returned and woke her up again as he came in.

Joni decided not to get up. The house remained quiet for the rest of the night.

In the morning, Joni talked to Karl again about his behavior on their way into town. He remained silent. That evening he did not come home. Joni wasn't going to call his folks, but the following morning was awakened by their call.

"Hi Joni. Just calling to see how things are going. We got your letter." Donald was chipper. "We've gotten information on what we will do here if we can get Karl to come home for help."

"He's gone again," said Joni, "but, I think it's only a matter of time before he's back.

He doesn't want to be on the street anymore."

"Oh, no," Elaine and Donald said in unison. There was a disappointed pause and then.

"Don't look for him," Elaine shot in her feisty way. "If he comes back, fine, but don't waste your time looking for him."

"I won't, "Joni assured them. "From now on, it's up to him to make a move."

"This has to end," said Donald. "I'm on medication over this. What is it going to take for him to realize he needs help?"

"I don't know, Donald," Joni was wobbling between washing her hands of the situation and needing to see it to completion. She was tired, but she also knew she had to find real closure to be truly done with this. Donald was getting on her nerves with his constant fear and depression. Elaine was supporting Joni and her need to be a mother to her own son, and she was simultaneously holding up both ends of the relationship with her husband. It was because of Elaine that Joni kept any hope at all alive at this point. She marveled at how differently she had felt in the beginning; as if it was Donald who would pull the whole thing through. There seemed almost to be a seesaw of dedication between them over the months, but for now, Elaine was on the up side. The truth was that they were both dedicated parents, but the toll of this ordeal had tossed each about in turn. They ended the conversation and Joni sighed to herself as she hung up. A moment of reflection, then she was off to prepare her day.

She had invited a friend, Debbie to dinner. Debbie had been the cleaning lady at the office and she was full of interest in the new age and metaphysical. A young and pretty woman, she was far from the stereotypical downtrodden scullery maid. She had well styled shoulder length brown hair and dancing deep brown eyes. Her skin was flawless and figure could just as easily have been that of well-kept royalty as of a hard working woman. Joni was looking forward to the evening and

221

answering Debbie's questions at length regarding Buddhism. There had never been enough time or privacy at the office to discuss the philosophy in depth and Debbie was hungry for information. It gave Joni a great reason for a miniature party, as well.

She had already told Debbie about Karl staying at her house and now cautioned her that he might be there for dinner as well. "That's fine with me," said Debbie brightly. "I'd actually like to meet him!"

"Great!" Joni had said, "Then it's all set. It will be fun...and if Karl doesn't come home, then that will be okay, too."

But, Karl did come home. Once again he had pulled through his darkness and was feeling light and loving again. He startled Joni as he appeared at the door. "Hi!" he said smiling and handed her a card at the same time. "I'm sorry about not coming home and I do want to marry you."

Joni was thrown off guard by this statement, so she opened the card. It was a 'sorry I haven't written' card and inside Karl had written: "Joni, sorry for the inconveniences I caused you. God had some important information he could communicate in no other way. I'll look forward to a bright future with you as companion. Love, Karl - PS: This card seemed to fit somehow."

"Well, thanks, Karl," Joni said as she welcomed him home with a hug. She was certain that he wasn't serious about the marriage or companion part, but was saying what he thought she wanted to hear. Nonetheless, she was glad he was back and she quickly filled him in on the fact that they were having a guest for dinner.

Karl was more than agreeable. He went to take a shower as Joni set the table. Debbie arrived and they ate and

222

talked amiably. Karl was on the quiet side, but not sullen. As Joni served him Debbie watched the interaction carefully.

"He really appreciates the way you treat him with such respect", she would later tell Joni. "I was amazed at how you treated him. I think it would help in my marriage!" Joni was surprised by this, but thankful for the observation. It made her feel very warm to have been seen through such loving eyes. They shared a bit about Buddhism that night, she and Debbie; and they spent some time chanting together. It was a pleasant, bonding type of evening.

After Debbie left, Karl asked Joni if she would like to go for a walk. She was happy to get out into the fresh night air with him. They walked their usual route around a country block or two and came back refreshed.

"I'm working on a play!" Karl had told her as he got out his paper and pens to write.

"Good for you, Karl," she said in reply. Joni was satisfied to get back about her own business. It felt fine for Karl to be writing quietly and busily in the living room as she finished her chores and settled into bed with the TV. She had lost the battle of insisting that he sleep, but he had compensated by being quiet and respectful. Some nights he did sleep, but the cycle was unpredictable at best.

Kevin called that night. "How are you, sweetie?" Joni asked as usual. "I'm fine," he said, "just have an ear infection, but I went to the doctor." "Do they have you on antibiotics?" she said with concern.

Kevin returned, "Oh, yeah. I didn't even stay home from school. They've got me on that pink stuff."

"Amoxicillin?"

"I guess so. Whatever that stuff is. Anyway, I'm going with Dad tomorrow to clean out the Cape Cod house and get it ready for the summer."

"Kevin, you should be resting. You've had a cold all winter and now an ear infection, too! Isn't there any way you can just stay home and rest?"

"I don't think so, Mom. Don't worry. I'll be fine."

Joni was worried. Kevin had been almost constantly sick with a cold or low grade infection of some kind when he lived with his dad and step mother. They had a policy of making him drink milk everyday - even though he was obviously intolerant of it in Joni's eyes. It amazed her how he would clear up each time he visited her, but this was not a well-received message and just another minor frustration in a string of minor frustrations common to the separated parent. Life as usual. Par for the course. She had to let it go and keep her eye on the day when Kevin would be able to make his own decisions about the foods he ate and the rest he needed. She hoped that he wouldn't become conditioned to the fast-paced frenzy that was life with his dad. He had always been a child who needed his rest and benefited greatly from it. More than once he had come to visit since the custody change and after the first day listing all the activities he wanted to do, would collapse and "veg out" for a day or so. These were treasured quiet moments as Joni could actually feel him settle physically, mentally and spiritually back into himself. It wasn't something she discussed, but a mother's knowing. Often as she prayed across a continent, she would send the healing energy she knew her son needed. Mostly she felt she couldn't send enough.

As Joni hung up the phone Karl asked how Kevin was. "He's got an ear infection and they're making him clean out the Cape Cod house tomorrow!" She was exasperated. "They didn't even keep him home from school. The trip to Cape Cod is 3 hours each way!"

"Don't worry, "Karl reassured. "He'll be okay." "I know," said Joni, "It's just so frustrating..."
"He'll probably come and live with you anyway."

"I hope so," she finished as Karl went back to his writing.

On nights like this Joni almost forgot that Karl was sick. His encouragement and calm demeanor was just enough reassurance to let her feel as though she had been heard. It was nicer than the talking she had done to the walls, by far. If the good and gentle Karl could always be, she could easily live with him forever.

Days later it was again time to pen another letter to his parents.

March 28, 1994

Dear Donald and Elaine,

Karl did return. I stopped by on Sunday (he left early A.M.) at the café where he hangs out around 3 PM...asked if he wanted to come home he said no. When I asked it he was coming home later he said he didn't know yet. I said ok and left. He showed up around 7 PM...just in time for dinner, although he wasn't too hungry. He was in a happy mood. Said he felt much better and had had a productive day. We talked about his play...I gave him some suggestions for angles in how to approach his idea and he really enjoyed the exchange. I made sure to make physical contact with him during this "up" time, so that he can feel less afraid of it. He is still not responding, but did not seem disturbed at my touching him. He slept well last night (in the chair) and still seemed quite positive this morning.

He's been asking about things that are going on in the world. I've told him about 'The tragedy of the day' per the news...shootings, auto accidents, the tornado in Alabama. It's not fun stuff, but I feel as though it's a sign that he's looking outward a bit more. He had no idea about the shooting of the Japanese Exchange student that happened some time ago in Florida (? If I remember right) and the recent killing of 2 more Japanese students...and how there are now traveling advisories for tourists in this country. He didn't realize that he had been 'walking the tracks' the same time Polly Klaas was abducted, nor that they caught Richard Allen Davis two months later and recovered her body. A world spotlight on Petaluma and yet lost on him.

Also, Elaine, I think you were right again when you said you thought that perhaps he wanted to be 'connected' to Buddhist practice...he asked me if I was going to "do nam myoho" last night as I went to do prayers...I said yes and had him say the whole phrase, "Nam Myoho Renge Kyo" he seemed happy to learn it. This morning he again asked me and pronounced the phrase...but when he asked for an explanation of it, as I told him, he wrote notes and also scribbled YH YH YH. I think that he is still afraid to give up his "mantram" as he calls it. But, the good news is he has said Nam Myoho Renge Kyo voluntarily...and it's taken 4 months for this to occur. In Buddhist teachings Shariputra was the last disciple to attain enlightenment - because he was the most intelligent and kept relying on his mind...it's the biggest barrier because enlightenment cannot be intellectually held! Anyway, Karl is definitely smart and stubborn...both should be with capital 's's!

We'll see if this goes anywhere, but it's a joy to be with him when he's feeling happy and sharing!

My heart-felt feeling is that should things go badly for him with me, he will come home to you. I feel that he now has regained a sense of home and comfort that he will not easily give up

226

again. The question remains...how far?.., how long? I feel "on top" of things again after having "lost it" on Saturday. The best scenario would still be for him to request help either here or there. I hope that not too much more of his life will go by before this happens.

He has become comfortable at the local café where he writes and apparently has met the owner. The situation could be similar to Steamers, I guess. He did say this morning that he might write a poem about the East-West Café and give it to the owner for his wall. I think this is another positive sign.

I continue to encourage his writing, with gentle hints that he may want to try to balance out his life a bit more. That's probably the most difficult thing for him to comprehend, because from what I've learned about his life, he has fairly consistently been compulsive about whatever "phase" he was in at the time. As if to perfect something or some aspect of his life to the exclusion of all others was to be worthy, holy and right.

It's not far from any other genius, it's just over the line of mental health. I will also encourage him to take responsibility for his actions...as we know that his deferring to an outside entity is also a deep disturbance. If he could see that it is, and choose to correct it...WOW! What a life he could have...and he wouldn't have to change much at all...just come out of his delusion. Let's hope. Let's pray.

I'm still stronger than the problem thanks to the support and encouragement I receive from both of you. I had a thought the other day that perhaps Karl's illness has served a function in deepening the relationship between the two of you. Most couples would have long ago crumbled under the strain. Perhaps someday if you feel it's true, you could relate this to Karl and ease the guilt he will surely feel as he recovers.

As for me, you have both helped me in terms of my relationship with my parents. It hasn't been a bad one, but there's been a level of 'if they don't ask, don't tell.' Through helping you to see Karl as he is, I feel I'm healing some of my own mystery with my parents. They may not like all that they see in me, but I now feel it's okay for me to be different. Thank you! Love, Joni

She wrote in her diary four days later: March 26

Today is the anniversary of Grandma's death. I miss grandma terribly at times like now. It's one of those more difficult mornings for me. (She was deep in a sort of nondescript despair) Karl has gone off to write at his café in town - he's invited me to come by & visit him - seems to be reaching out- but, strangely, I feel like avoiding him. What is going on? Feeling like I've scraped bottom - his writing is all so negative towards me. He calls me a witch and a temptress. He calls me stupid and unkind (in his writing). He wants so much to be right - when I am weak - I feel like giving in - my karma is a trap today. Thank you, Gohonzon.

        The day passed slowly and by the very next day Joni was feeling alive and happy again. Her time away from Karl was a valuable and necessary rejuvenation. Her leadership duties with the Buddhist organization were also a saving grace. She was able to stay sane due to the many other responsibilities she had taken on in life. It wasn't the first time that she would remember Viktor Frankl's philosophy on treating depression…if someone is depressed…they need more responsibility…they need to care for someone else. As a survivor of two Nazi concentration camps, his opinion carried lots of weight with Joni. She had read his book, <u>Man's Search For Meaning,</u> several times in her life and wanted very much to be able to someday practice his type of psychotherapy, Logotherapy. From the root word logo –which translates to 'meaning'. If one can find meaning in their suffering they can not only survive, but thrive. Joni's Buddhist practice was very

228

much in line with his philosophy or vice versa…and she was grateful for that. Was it because of his book or just a natural consequence that she too, was constantly searching for meaning in life? As long as she was able to derive meaning from the process she was endeavoring through, she could succeed. When the times of self-pity and self-flagellation rolled in, she would lose ground again and become enmeshed in the insanity. She knew, though, that even if it looked minuscule to the naked eye, she was making progress. After weak days she rebounded with triple strength and fortitude.

By now friends would ask her with searching eyes how 'things' were going. She wasn't sure most of the time exactly how much they wanted to hear. But, the best of it was that friends brought her books to read or passages about others with the same types of illness.

"I thought you might like to read this," said Joni's friend, Susan, as she offered her copy of Twilight, by Elie Wiesel. "It's about a guy who thinks he's Jesus. Actually it's based on true stories. It might help you with Karl."

"Thanks!" Joni was hopping into the car as the book found its way to the back seat. "I'd really be interested to read it," she assured Susan, although she wasn't quite sure when or if she'd have time. The book rode around in the back seat of the car for a week or more before Joni had a chance during a lunch break to pick it up and open it. Some of the passages hit home so well, that she felt a part of her coming home. It was light and entertaining, not a dire commiseration of the dreaded 's-word'.

She photocopied pages and highlighted the parts that delighted her the most. One was, "Who says that madmen cannot help the "sane"? Often their madness consists precisely in their wish to save others. Raphael has met his share of madmen. He owes them some of his most exalted moments."

She was transformed as she read and followed this Raphael in his odyssey through the sane and the insane; the free vs. the confined.

Toward the end of the book he asks, "What did he want me to learn here? That human beings are frail? That their truths change? That there is one truth for the judges and another for the judged? That doubt is as necessary to faith as air is to fire? That there is only a fine line between innocence and guilt? Madmen frighten me, but not as much as those who push them into madness."

Joni could relate. She also feared her involvement could do more harm than good. She remembered Charlie, her ex-boss at the Alcoholism Association she had worked at years before. Charlie was a recovering alcoholic who had been sober for 16 years at that time. He was in demand with helping others and giving guidance to those struggling with their addiction. He always said he prayed, "Lord, if I can't help them, please just don't let me hurt them." Apropos, thought Joni; something well worth remembering and repeating.

Other things began to crowd her mind, though. It was coming on spring now. The weather was warmer and soon there would be no more rain for the summer. It was clear that a change had to happen and soon it would be upon her. Kevin was coming for Easter break. Joni decided to talk with Elaine a bit the next time she called. "Things are going well, "she said, "but, Karl doesn't really have any intention of getting work or help. I'm feeling this is really bad for him. He makes himself dependent and then resents the fact that he is. Kevin is coming in a few weeks, too…"

"Your son has to come first," Elaine was thinking out loud. "I think we should make Karl's last day next week. He either gets help or gets out. We need to force the situation."

230

"I think you're right, Elaine. I'm just not sure what he'll do. The weather is getting better and I have a few weeks before Kevin comes…"

"Joni, I can't thank you enough for what you've done already. I really think that if you make a deadline Karl will come through. If not, well, you've done what you can. Your own son has to come first now."

"Thank you, Elaine," Joni was beginning to cry…"It's hard to see him go out on the street again after all of this time and effort. I really wanted to see this thing through, but you're absolutely right, my son does have to come first - he always has, especially when he's here. I have always dropped everything during his visits; they're so precious to me. And, I want him to feel free to choose, if he does want to come back to live, too."

"Joni, it's going to be okay, remember?" Elaine was crying now, too. "We're going to get a full miracle!"

"Yes," Joni sobbed.

"Just pick a day and stick with it - maybe Friday?"

"Well, I'd like to give him notice - just in case it inspires him to do something. I also know it's harder for him on the weekends…so I'll say two weeks from Monday…that will be the 11th."

"I'm going to keep praying for our miracle, Joni." "Me, too, Elaine. Thank you!"

As she hung up the phone Joni felt relieved and anxious and winded. Whew! It was really going to come to a head. This was scary, but having Elaine as a back-up would help. She'd have to go through with it now. There would be no turning back.

231

That night she told Karl that he would have to either get help, get a job, or at least sign up for financial aid in order to stay. She told him that she would help him through, if he decided to get counseling and that he would always be welcomed to come and eat, but that he would have to take some steps toward health in order to stay. He agreed to what she said, but as the days ticked by, it was obvious that he had no intention of changing a single aspect of his life.

"Did you get your tickets, honey?"

"Yes, mom," said Kevin. "I talked to Dad about moving out this year, but he says that if I do I can never come back because I'll be too far behind in school."

"I don't believe that. Kevin, you have to do what you feel is necessary for your life no matter how your Dad and I feel. I don't want you to come here to live just to make me happy…although you know I do want you to be here. I really want you to do what you feel is best for you. It might be difficult if you got here and didn't like it…you would have to finish out the school year at least…"

"Oh I know, that, Mom. That wouldn't be a problem…if I made a mistake, I know I'd have to finish the year, but I don't think I would hate it…I might try next year."

"Kev', you know whatever you decide, I'll support your decision. I want you here, but your Dad loves you, too. He also has more money and things wouldn't come as easily here, you know…"

"I know, Mom, believe me, I know. But, that's not bothering me. The part that bothers me is that Dad and Ellie are going to be hurt or mad if I come out."

"I know, honey."

"I just wish they could say what you say…that they would support my decision. It's just so hard…"

"Honey, if it's too hard, don't force the issue. You only have two more years of school left anyway."

"I know, but I don't think I can take it here two more years, that's just it!"

"Well, when you come out for your visit, let's see how you feel. You may spend some time with Billy and get an idea of how the high school is and stuff. Hey, you two would be in the same school for once, wouldn't you?"

"Yeah. That would be cool, too. Well, I gotta go. I'll call you before I come out." "Okay, honey. I can't wait to see you!" Kevin flipped into one of his favorite 'Jerky Boys' voices, "say yer prayers, jerky…."

"you, too, jerky…I love you," Joni laughed as she hung up the phone. Would there ever be a person she could enjoy as much as this kid? She truly wanted him to be happy…whether that meant living with her or not. She had prayed that he would return to live with her for almost 8 years now, and had all but given up hope that it would happen before he reached college age. She wanted to be hopeful, but then, she didn't want to get her hopes up too high. She wasn't even sure that she still knew how to be a full time mother, but she sure was willing to try.

Having Karl around had awakened her desire to mother again. She was happy doing dishes and laundry and especially learning how to cook again. The part of her that missed her boy had been submerged under other duties and activities. She had gone about, chin up and moving forward, not really letting the loneliness or pain set in for long. It was insanity she feared…that if she allowed herself to feel the pain of missing Kevin, she might never return to life itself. Counseling had helped, but Karl's presence in the house had uncovered something she thought might have been lost…her joy of caring for another. Something good was coming out of all this - something sane and real and beyond all rational explanation. She and Karl were taking turns helping each other to return to themselves. Joni wondered if he would ever understand how deep her appreciation was for that; and would he ever feel the same toward her? No matter, really, a healing was taking place for both of them…in different ways, perhaps, but happening nonetheless. And these were very old wounds, indeed.

"Even though the earth were flipped away with a finger; If there were someone who linked the heavens, should the tides cease to ebb and flow, or should the sun rise in the West, it could never happen that the prayers of the devotees of the Lotus Sutra would go unanswered."

On Prayer - Nichiren Daishonin

Chapter Thirteen Answered

April 5, 1994

Dear Donald & Elaine:

Once again writing to report...I am trying to gently, but firmly, make Karl face reality. Don't know if this will eventually work, or if I am wasting my time. I know that he's been taking change out of my bedroom...he takes it when I'm doing gongyo (morning prayers) so, I took the change and hid it and left a note saying, "It's not okay to take without asking." On the coffee bag that he has hidden under his chair I left him a note that said, "It's not okay to steal." I know that this is a bit childish, but he doesn't seem to be able to handle direct confrontation. He runs away, lets the situation cool and then returns...so nothing ever gets resolved. The only other recourse is extreme anger, but that is destructive, too.

I realized this morning that the reason people get so mad at him is because underneath he is seething with anger, but he never expresses it...therefore, just being around him when he's depressed makes one feel anger. Well, it's a theory.

235

Sunday night when we went for our walk he started talking about how he hoped apes never learned to talk because they wouldn't have anything intelligent to say and how humans are so superior to animals, etc. I told him I felt his constant categorization between good & evil, better or lesser, etc. was a problem and that he needed to have more balance in his life. I also told him that he thinks the intellect is the supreme source of wisdom because that's where he lives...in his head. I told him that he will never be able to fully know wisdom until he can integrate and experience the world. I also told him that he needed to come out and join the rest of us, but that he thinks he's too good for us. He took it in, but didn't comment directly.

After a few minutes a car came by and he started rambling about how it was a machine that was made of steel, plastic and glass and that we raped the earth just to have transportation to go places we didn't need to go, etc., etc. I chimed in, "That's what I like about you, you're always so cheerful!"

He said, "That's the cheerful picture...do you want to know the bleak picture?"

I said, "No! I've been living with the bleak picture for four months!" He laughed and started sing-songing "I've been living with the bleak picture...."

Last night I was on the phone for a long time with Tom, my co-leader for the SGI (our Buddhist Organization). Karl went out for his walk and came back...I was still on the phone so he went out again. When I said goodnight he barked, "See ya." I asked why he was angry and he told me I was making things up. I stood silently in the kitchen watching him and trying to understand for about 15 minutes. He didn't say anything more, so I went to bed. I felt at the time that he was very tired, and not feeling well due to hay fever, etc. and that he really resents being at my house. I understand all of that. As I'm writing this,

236

though, it occurs to me that he may have been jealous of my phone call and/or resentful that I didn't go walking with him.

I watched him from my bed as I have many times. When he doesn't close the drapes in front of his desk, I can easily see his reflection in the window…he sat at his desk his eyes trying to close and his head bobbing. Every time he let his chin drop he'd try to sit up again fighting sleep harder than any child…he does this for at least half an hour. It is pitiful to watch. If only he could overcome his fear of sleep or his belief that this is a holy vigil that he keeps!

He overheard my conversation with my friend, Fran on Sunday night, too. He asked about it last night and I explained how Fran has manic depressive illness, too (I let the 'too' slide by; he didn't comment) and that she is on Elavil. I explained to him that she gets overwhelmed with problems and calls me crying and how I talk to her, sometimes sharply to get her back on track. I also let him know that by the time I got off the phone she felt as though she had 'broken through' some of her karma. She has been practicing Buddhism for 5 years and has come a long way. Her whole family has manic-depression to some degree. Karl is not stupid, as we know, so I'm sure he took the hint. But, it's still hard for him to face this reality.

This morning he was very depressed. Partially due to the fact that he slept, partially (my guess) due to the fact that he can feel things changing. I'm not letting so much go by. He also, I think, feels trapped, because he doesn't want to live on the street and has promised that he'll never again take off without calling me. He knows he's at the end of that game and that if he leaves again, it's for good. He also knows that we all feel he needs help, and I think on some level he may be facing that, too. He told me the other night that he was confused as to where he was on his story about the Vikings. He couldn't quite follow what he had written. He asked me to read some of it and my suggestion was that perhaps he could intersperse some narrative with the verses...he replied, "You're silly." So I dropped it.

I expect tonight when I pick him up he'll be happy again or at least pleasant. His depressions don't seem to last too long. If he were able to give up his belief that sleep is harmful, he could even out his moods a lot just with a regular regimen. The question is, does his lack of sleep cause the depression/mania or does the manic-depressive illness cause the lack of sleep? Does the belief that sleep is harmful come from paranoia/schizophrenia, or does the belief and practice cause schizophrenia? At any rate, Karl is his own biggest block to happiness whether the cause be organic, psychological, spiritual or a combination of the above. I'm trying to remember to respect his struggle more than pity it. Thanks for your help!

Love, Joni

"Want to go for a walk?" Karl was asking Joni as she put the groceries away. "That sounds great!" She was thankful for the diversion. It was nice to have someone who encouraged her to leave the house and walk...because the housework never really got done, anyway. As they walked she was lost in her own thoughts. It had long ceased to be a romantic walk, holding hands. Karl now kept space between them, but Joni could feel he enjoyed the companionship, too.

Out of the blue Karl began to sing at the top of his lungs...to the tune of Jingle Bells he sang "Nam myo ho..ren ge kyo nam myoho renge kyo oh! Nam myo ren ge kyo nam myoho renge kyo!" and then burst into laughter. Joni laughed, too and as she did he continued to sing alternating between song and laughter as they walked through the neighborhood. Joni's first thought was that he would disturb the neighbors, but it struck her so funny to hear him sing that she couldn't even shush him. Inside her heart was smiling, too, because she knew that even as a taunt or joke, he had made the cause of

238

chanting Nam Myoho Renge Kyo and this could only do him good.

After dinner Joni finished up the dishes and got a tray ready for Karl as had become their habit. She would brew a pot of tea and bring him the pot, a cup and saucer, napkin and a small plate of cookies on a tray before she went to bed. He would seldom stop his writing, but would always thank her sincerely. On this night, however, as she retreated finishing up a few last things in the kitchen before bed, he called out to her in a soft and gentle voice, "Good night, Nam myo…"

At the sink, Joni's heart twinged. It was the sweetest thing she had ever heard and she stopped short of a tear as she replied with a smile, "Good night, Renge Kyo." She felt her voice emanate from deep within her chest and float gently out to him. There was a wave of warmth that connected them. They looked at each other and smiled from across the room. Karl knew he had hit a winner and he felt proud and loved. The moment hung in the air while they savored it.

Joni was feeling the pain that comes with ambivalence. Did she really need to go through with it? Send him out on the 11th? Was there a miracle around just one more corner? Part of her knew that she would have to stick by her decision, but part of her wanted to back down. In her journal she wrote to herself, "What is my true prayer? I have to remember that it is for my own and for Karl's true happiness. I must not slander my own life in favor of his, yet I must retain true compassion. Thich Nhat Hanh says in Peace Is Every Step, "When you understand you can't help but love." How true! "

She decided that she should talk to Karl as openly as possible to try and get him to understand the situation he was facing. She told him that she was feeling as though she was ready to have a relationship with a man.

239

"That's fine with me," said Karl not batting an eye or raising his gaze from his work.

"It's not that easy," Joni knew she was in trouble now. She really hadn't thought that a meaningful discussion would come out of this, but she didn't quite expect this, either. "Karl, I can't go on with my life while you're living here…"

Karl had put on his radio headphones. Joni took a step toward him and he got up and bolted out the door. The routine had become very old. She no longer missed a beat in thinking he might really be gone. Sure enough, he was back 45 minutes later.

Daimoku was what Joni needed most now. She got an opportunity the next day at work. She was at her client's studio to work on his books and he was out of town. She chanted as she worked all day…seven hours. Wisdom was always her number one request…this day was no different. She needed the wisdom to know what to do next.

Karl's behavior over the next few days was consistent with what had gone before.

He would be light and cooperative and sweet alternating with closed and dark and silent moods. Joni knew that this was symptomatic of his disease, but a part of her still held out a glimmer of hope that a lucid moment would prevail and that she would be able to get him to help. The glimmer was now flickering dangerously on the brink of extinction as the last day of Karl's stay drew near.

"You know, if you'll get any kind of help…you can stay…", she offered.

The phone rang. It was his parents. Joni felt as though it was a call from the Warden to the dead man's cell. "Yes, he's

240

here," she said as she handed the phone to Karl. "It's your parents."

Karl took the phone, "Okay," he said. "It's possible...I love you, too...." and then he hung up.

"What did they say?" Joni asked.

"They just said the same thing they've been saying...that I could go back there."

"Do you think you will, Karl?"

"Maybe, but I don't really think so. Besides, I have to do what God tells me to do. It has nothing to do with what I want."

"If you get help, Karl, you don't have to go back. I'll stand by you 'til you can make it on your own..."

Karl had gone back to his chair. The discussion was closed. Joni stopped herself short again. Don't buy into it, she thought. Do what you need to do. Let it go.

On April 10 she wrote in her journal:

Tonight will be Karl's last night here. He's chosen to return to the street rather than seek any kind of help or assistance. He may return to his parents, but this has yet to be seen. I expect he will try to pick up another woman to care for him. He writes vile things about me - how evil I am - calling me witch and despising me in every possible way. How sad that this belies our deep connection, but that all is reversed.

Wisdom, Gohonzon, I need Wisdom today. Joni prayed as she did her morning prayers. She wanted to leave no stone unturned, but now it was just a matter of minutes before she would be throwing Karl out. She had told him that he could come back for meals and showers a couple times per week, but that he wasn't going to be able to return to live. As she finished her prayers she felt a calm strength come over her. She would be fine. She would summon wisdom somehow.

As they got into the car the calm gave way to deep feelings of compassion. As she drove Karl remained silent. *This is my last chance*, she thought to herself. "What are your plans, Karl?", she asked, not really expecting an answer.

"I'm not telling you," he sneered like a brat kid.

Joni snapped. "Yeah, I'm just a witch!"

"Yeah," he answered.

"I was the only one who took you in and cared for you and listened to you. But, that's bad to you, isn't it Karl? People who kick you and spit on you are good in your mind, but people who care are bad..." She was hot as he cut her off.

"Just take me to the J.C.," he demanded. "You don't have to say anything." He was sneering and brushing her off like a half-dead bug.

"I'LL SAY WHATEVER I WANT!" Joni was not backing down. As she maneuvered a turn onto the main street, Karl put on his radio headset. Joni grabbed it off his head with one hand.

He grabbed it back and then punched her in the arm. He couldn't stop. He just kept pounding and pounding on her as she drove.

I can't believe he's hitting me, she thought. She had come to a calm place within her that made this feel like a dream. I've got to pull over.... The car was now slowing to a snail's pace, but Joni couldn't see to the side of the road because Karl kept hitting her.

He took a break and she saw an open space at the beginning of the block. She pulled the car over sloppily as the car behind her swerved in anger to get around. The people in the car looked at her as Karl threw a few last punches, but they did nothing. Karl was yelping as he delivered these last few blows, "God damn it...God damn it God damn it." But the sound he made was more like a child's cry than that of an angry man. Joni turned and looked at him as he scrambled out of the car. She was not hurt. She felt a calm and a strange joy as she called out to him.

"That's good, Karl! It's good that you got angry!" He looked ashen as he gathered his things from the sidewalk and started to run away.

Joni sat for a moment to catch her breath. She was utterly calm as she felt her arm move to shift into drive again. It was good that he got mad, she felt. If he got mad enough at how his life is going, he could get desperate enough to seek help!

Do I call the police? She thought to herself as she drove to work. *What good will that do? He'll just be in jail with a record and maybe still won't get help. What if he could get help that way, though?* She was sure of one thing, he wasn't going to get another chance to hurt her. Joni's winter coat had provided good protection. Only a few of the punches had hit her chin slightly. Just her arm and shoulder were bruised and her silver bracelet was mangled. She had been protected for sure.

"Elaine, I'm sorry to be bothering you at work," she began...and then her throat closed up as she squeaked, "Karl's out and he hit me. I don't want to call the police." Elaine asked for details and Joni gave her a detailed explanation of the past hour's experience.

"Joni! I can't believe it." Elaine's voice was a mixture of disbelief, anger and sorrow. "I need to make a phone call and then I'll call you back. Are you sure you're okay?"

Joni hung up and went back to work. She was aware of her body and aware of her face throbbing slightly. *This is a reminder*, she thought of her pain. *This is to keep you from forgetting just how much help Karl needs.*

Several hours later the phone rang, "Good Afternoon, Dr. Trowbridge's office, "Joni said in her best professional voice.

"Joni, I have someone I want you to talk to." It was Elaine. "Are you at a place where you can talk for a bit?"

"Yes, just let me pick this up in the back, office, though, Elaine. Just a minute." Joni put the call on hold as she went back to the Dr.'s office. She was the only one there, but the office shared a waiting room with another physician. She often used the back office when she needed to be private on the phone.

"Okay, Elaine. I'm here," said Joni.

"Joni, I want you to talk to Donna. She's a friend and a judge out here. I've told her what happened with Karl."

"Hi Joni. I'm Donna. Elaine has told me about what happened today. She says you don't want to go to the police…"

"Well, I just don't want Karl to have a felony record over this. He needs help, and from all I've seen of the system out here, there's no way going to jail is going to get him any closer to help. If it would help him, I would do it…but, what do you think about it?"

"Joni, Karl has hit you now, right?" "Yes."

"Well, unfortunately, that is a bad sign. In cases like Karl's, once that threshold of violence is crossed, they don't go back. In other words, it will be easier for him to become violent again now and this could even escalate. You cannot take him back in again."

"I wasn't planning on it. I feel more sorry for him than scared, though."

"I understand. I know that you're not seriously hurt, but I just want you to know that this is not going to get any better until Karl does get help."

"I understand. Thank you."

Elaine got on the line again. "Joni, thank you for all you've done. You may hear from Karl again, but don't let him come back. Go to the police and report this, Joni. It may actually be the godsend we're looking for. It may be that with a police report on file, Karl can get help."

"Okay, Elaine. After talking with you and Donna, I'm convinced it's what I should do.

I'll go on my way home from work today."

"Good!"

"I hope you're right. I hope that this turns out to be the catalyst we've needed to get Karl to help."

Joni was not convinced that the police would do anything, but if she explained why she was reporting the incident, perhaps they could give her some answers. She wondered if Karl would get taken in somewhere else and just repeat this process over and over ad infinitum.

"Let me know if Karl contacts you, Elaine," she said as they hung up. "You, too, Joni. And thanks again for all you've done."

I hope it's enough, thought Joni to herself. The worst that could happen now would be for nothing to change. Something had to give. There had been too much effort put out for all of this to just wash down the drain.

On her way home from work, Joni drove into the police station to report the morning's incident. As she described what happened to the officer he told her that there would be no charge filed. She had initiated/aggravated the situation by grabbing the headphones from Karl. In other words, she had assaulted him...so there was no case, except that they would put a report in a file. Joni gave her silver bracelet as evidence. Because she had no serious, visible bruises to show, the officer was generally uninterested in pursuing much detail of her story.

Well, she thought as she left the station. That was pretty much wasted time. I've gone and reported this thing and there's is nothing at all that will come of it. So much for our idea that this could bring help into Karl's life.

"What is it going to take?" Donald was exasperated on the other end of the line as Joni described her encounter with the police.

"I know, Donald. I tried to tell the officer about the fact that Karl needed help...and about his previous shoplifting charges. It all was a wash because I grabbed the headphones.

246

But, I'll tell you something, I personally think it was a good thing that Karl lost control because it may scare him enough to think that he could get arrested for it."

"That's a thought," said Donald as Elaine 'uummed' on the extension. "I just can't believe this system, though. Do you know that I am on anti-depressant medication over this?"

"I know, "said Joni softly glad that he couldn't see her rolling her eyes.

"What is it going to take for this thing to come to an end? I just don't know if we can go through any more of this…"

"Yes, we can and we will," said Elaine with a firm, but supportive voice. "We're going to see our full miracle come through. We'll do whatever it takes…"

"It's really just a matter of time," Joni tried to sound reassuring. The truth was, and they all knew it, but were afraid to verbalize it, that anything could happen to Karl out on the street. He might also end up in jail for a very long time with no prospect of real help. He might be lost to them forever; that was the truth none of them could say.

Defeat encircled her as she hung up the phone. Would these parents be spared a grisly end to this madness? Thoughts paraded through her mind of possible outcomes. Would he be found dead? If so, would she be notified? Would he hook up with another woman and become even more violent? Would he commit other crimes and end up in jail? Or would he actually come to his senses and decide to go for help? She knew that she would have to wait and let it unfold in its own time. That was the part she hated the most. The not knowing. Her feet led her to her altar, where she knelt down to do her evening prayers and once again chant for this young man to be returned to happiness and health.

Her tears flowed freely as she faced the Gohonzon (scroll) and chanted. This can't end in defeat, she determined. It's *got* to work out, somehow. I won't accept anything less than the full potential of this being to his enlightened state! She wasn't going to let the negative pictures of possible outcomes into her mind. Instead she would continue to focus on a picture of Karl as a healthy adult…teaching a lecture at a university and laughing about the days he had endured as Jesus. She forced herself to feel the joy of that scene and forsake the others that clamored to break through to her consciousness. You can create your own reality, she had read that somewhere. Well, one thing was certain; dwelling on the negative would only cause more of it. She was tired enough without giving in to a draining mental program as well. So she chanted, and then became weary and went to bed and slept very, very soundly.

The next day was sunny and her mother was hanging clothes out to dry in the courtyard that separated their ends of the house. Joni blurted out, "Karl's gone for good," as she unexpectedly burst into tears. Her mother hugged her.

"You did all you could do. It's up to him now," she said softly. It was all the confirmation Joni needed. She was so thankful for her family's support through this most bizarre chapter. She also knew that if what the psychiatrists were saying was true, that Karl's violence could escalate…there was no way at all that she would have him in close proximity to her parents. She desperately wanted safety and security for them and as little impact as possible from her own crazy life. She was conflicted as always about the situation, but felt that she had dodged a bullet. She would never confess that Karl had hit her to her mother. It wasn't worth worrying her.

"For virtually any other serious sickness, a patient who felt similar devastation would be lying flat in bed, possibly sedated and hooked up to the tubes and wires of life-support systems, but at the very least in a posture of repose and in an isolated setting. His invalidism would be necessary, unquestioned and honorably attained. However, the sufferer from depression has no such option and therefore finds himself, like a walking casualty of war, thrust into the most intolerable social and family situations. There he must, despite the anguish devouring his brain, present a face approximating the one that is associated with ordinary events and companionship. He must try to utter small talk and be responsive to questions, and knowingly nod and frown and, God help him, even smile. But it is a fierce trial attempting to speak even a few simple words."

- William Styron --<u>Darkness Visible A Memoir Of Madness</u>

Chapter Fourteen   No Answer

Joni tried to contemplate the turmoil that Karl must have been engulfed in. She could feel his pull, that he wanted her to find him. She knew that if she looked, she would find him, but the gentle throbbing of her face and arm reminded her...not this time. As the days trudged by hour by hour she prayed for him to get some help. The phone rang at work...no answer as she greeted the caller. She hung up quickly, feeling that it must be him, but not wanting to encourage conversation. It rang at home, still no answer on the other end. She felt her teeth clench as she gritted them against opposing forces within.

249

On April 12 she wrote:

Feeling sad this morning. I miss Karl and wish that things could have worked out - on the other hand, I know it's time for me to keep my family safe and move on to my own right relationship. My only fear is that I may have done more harm than good to Karl. I trust my instincts through the Gohonzon - but maybe should have walked away long ago. I know he wants to be here safe and warm, yet he can't choose to get well. Is it right for me to try to force him to health & what I see as happiness? Perhaps he would rather suffer as Mercedes mentioned when I called Sunday, "You'd think
people who have a lot of pain would want to be rid of it - but they don't - the more the better!" So true. She's so neat.

At a break in her day, she wrote to Karl's parents:

April 12, 1994

Dear Donald & Elaine:

Karl left behind his notebook which had his computer printouts of poetry. Most of them you've already seen, but I was interested to read the first page which states that he did go into Samadhi! This was written when he left in February as he also mentions that I cared for him during Samadhi and then we parted ways.

The rest of the copies are from a more recent notebook which I stole out of his backpack before he left. I don't like to do this kind of thing, but I felt I wanted to at least make copies of some of these and that I could return the book to him later. As you can see, his feelings toward me are hateful and condescending. Perhaps this is how he interprets my interference with his life...I do so wish that I could have either helped or walked away. My fear is that I may have caused him

250

more harm than good, but I have no ill feelings toward him. If he can have a happy life in spite of this, I wish it. If he is truly happier "serving" God, I apologize for my interference. My motivation has been the preservation of his life, which I felt was in danger, especially during the harsh winter months. For this I do not apologize...even though he has now assaulted me.

I will continue to pray for his recovery and happiness. I hope that he will someday be able to renew a friendship with me, but I do not expect he can forgive me for cornering him into feeling his most animalistic feelings. I hope that he can learn to accept both his negative and positive aspects and be able to balance out his personality. I truly respect his strength and courage and deeply love his tenderness and laughter. I will always cherish my time with him.

Let me know what else I can do, if anything. I expect he may call you before he calls me. It's agonizing to think of how he must be feeling.

Love, Joni

Later that evening she wrote:

Got a lot done at work, but it was not an easy day.

Thought about Karl and couldn't hold back tears several times.

She remembered as she wrote a new song had come onto the radio...it went, "how can I help you to say good-bye? It's okay to hurt and it's okay to cry. Come let me hold you and I will try...how can I help you to say good-bye?"

Tonight felt restless - so went to a movie to distract myself - it worked for an hour or so. Came home and went for a Karl and Joni walk - without Karl, of course. Cried my eyes out most of the way. I know I have to let go completely - the house still smells like him. Thank you, Gohonzon.

The pain of grieving gave way to a healing of sorts. Kevin was due to arrive on the 15th! Joni made his room ready. The 'Welcome Home' mylar banner was still in place over his bedroom door. She would have to shop for some of his favorite foods and put the finishing touches on his birthday gifts. The big present these days was to go shopping for clothes. Joni looked forward to the opportunity. Kevin always got such a charge out of his new duds. Despite this hustle and bustle she had made a date with Wayne from Steamers to exchange psychic readings.

She drove to Novato in the afternoon as the sun was losing its bite. Up a narrow canyon road and inching along a dirt bank to park, she was wary of the ditch just beyond the narrow shoulder of the road. Wayne and Ina's house was built on the side of this canyon...the lower side, so that as she parked the car near their parking platform, she could barely see the roof top beyond. It was a bit eerie at first, seeing a car parked on a cement platform that looked as though it might be suspended in air. The stairway to the left waited patiently for her to notice and she gingerly walked down three flights to a beautiful house below. The overgrowth of lush greenery and smell of honeysuckle and lavender gave the place a magical feel. It was a beauty she would long breathe in when thinking about these two.

Joni read for Wayne first. She was surprised to see in his cards that changes, big changes were brewing. She saw success for him, but when he asked point blank about the blockage between him and Ina, Joni blurted out, "She wants a baby."

"I don't think so," he mused. "We've talked about that and she doesn't really want kids...at least that's what she says...."

"Well, I could be wrong, "Joni gave her usual caveat in these situations, "But, wait and see. I definitely see a baby around her."

"Ok. Great!," said Wayne, "You've helped me with a lot of things...now it's your turn."

"I'm ready," said Joni with enthusiasm. She was looking forward to this experience. Wayne picked up on Karl's energy right away and told Joni that Karl did not want her to be there because he wanted to control her energy. He was 'cording' her...which meant psychically sucking her energy. Wayne worked to remove the blockage and as he asked Joni if she had questions, one sprung to her mind. "My Buddhist leader, Mr. Nagashima told me that Karl had come into my life to show me how to find my true partner. Do you have an idea of what he meant by that? Or do you see anything around that?"

A long silence ensued. Just then, the sliding glass door opened and Ina bounded in with her usual light. "Hi, how are you?" she asked Joni with a warm smile. Ina had a way of making everyone feel as they were the most important person on the planet when she spoke. "Oh, you're doing readings," she half-apologized as she went on and up the stairs to their room.

"Just a minute," said Wayne to Joni as he bounded after her. "Maybe Ina would like to trade a reading with you for a massage..."

"That would be fun, "Joni beamed as he disappeared around the corner and up the stairs.

A few minutes later Wayne returned, "I guess she's already got a client coming, but she'd love to do it another time."

"Oh, that's fine," said Joni and they spent a bit more time on her reading. Wayne told Joni that she needed to learn to run her own male energy. She needed to learn how to step out into the world…look at those feet! he had said…as if her tiny feet were a symbol of the point he was making. She listened, but she would need more time to digest what he was telling her; the heart of it felt right. Soon it was time for her to leave. It had been a pleasant experience. Joni really liked Wayne and was looking forward to getting to know Ina a little, better, too. She felt that they were really an ideal couple, so the thought that they were possibly splitting up was a disturbing one to her. From where she sat, she felt that Wayne would never find another Ina. But things look very different depending on whose shoes you are standing in. It was a true shock when several months later, Ina left him for another lover with whom she had become pregnant.

The exchange had left Joni feeling calmer and more centered. She was able to pick up and go on again and focus on the task at hand; preparing for Kevin's visit. As she drove to the airport the next day, she was filled with anticipation. Her son was like a shot in the arm whenever he visited. There was no longer any lag time before they felt at home with each other; in fact, it was as if they had never been apart.

"Yes, here it is," she said to the flight attendant as she offered her license as proof of her identity. She was already hugging Kevin, but rules were rules. "This will probably be one of the last times we'll have to go through that," she said to him as they walked toward the baggage claim area.

"Yeah, I told my Dad I didn't need to go as an unaccompanied minor this time, but he insisted."

"Pretty funny for a guy who wanted you to fly alone at age 8, huh?" "Yeah, well, you know him, Ma."

Kevin hadn't grown tremendously since his visit in December, but something about him seemed so much more grown up. Joni was happy just to be near him again, knowing that they would have time to talk and be together and just be for a time.

"I'll get that," Kevin said as he grabbed his heavy duffel bag and threw it onto the rented cart.

"Ok, honey," said Joni as she realized that he was stronger and quite a bit taller than she now. It felt good to her. She knew that he was able to take care of himself in many ways. What was somewhat astounding, though, was that he was now becoming capable of taking care of her, too. They stopped at McDonald's on their way home, which had become their 'coming home from the airport' tradition. The place had been remodeled and Kevin complained, "Why did they have to go and change it?"

"It's much better, don't you think?" Joni was smiling at his Jerky Boys voice.

"Yeah, it's nicer, but I liked the old, cruddy, funky look…it's just not the same. I've been comin' here all a dese years…and dey gotta go and change stuff on me while I'm like away…" He had lapsed into his Brooklyn accent and Joni was chuckling as she ordered.

The drive home was the usual pleasant exchange and Kevin made no secret of the fact that he was glad that Karl was gone. Joni was not about to tell him about the final 'incident' with Karl, but did caution Kevin that he might call or try to come back and that he was on the street, but she didn't know where. Soon after they pulled into the driveway Kevin was off like a

255

shot to Billy's. It was such a great inexplicable benefit that he had had a friend right across the street for all of these years. Joni knew that it leant continuity to his visits and she was more grateful than anyone could ever know.

It was a fairly early night to bed. They were both tired... Kevin from traveling for 12 hours door to door, Joni from working and driving a 4 hour round trip. It was the good kind of tired, though. The kind that makes you feel happy to have a clean bed and rest knowing loved ones are near.

The ring of the telephone woke Joni as she slept a bit late into the morning. She bolted up, so that the ring would not wake Kevin.

"Joni," the voice on the other end was sobbing. *Oh my God, thought Joni. What has happened?* She knew that it was Donald crying, she braced herself, eyes closed tightly for the news. Elaine was on the extension, and she was crying, too.

"Donald, what happened?" asked Joni, eyes still clenched shut as if to soften the blow that would soon assault her ears.

"He's coming home, Joni. He's coming home! He called this morning and we're getting a ticket arranged for him!"

"Oh, Donald!" said Joni, now crying herself. "That's such good news. I can't believe it! We've won!"

"Yes," said Elaine, "it's our miracle! Finally! We can't thank you enough!"

"Well, thank you, too... I couldn't have done it without you - you know that!" Joni's mind was racing now to details... were they celebrating prematurely? What if he backed out at the last minute?

Donald read her mind. "Of course, until we actually see him get off the plane, there's no telling if this is really real. But we're going to make it so that he has to go to the airport and get the ticket and he can't cash it in or anything."

"I could get him to the airport, if need be...," Joni was more than willing, she still hoped the shred of hesitancy wasn't obvious in her voice.

"I asked him that," Donald continued," he says he has enough to take the airporter down to the city...do you think that's right? Anyway, I asked if he wanted you to take him and he said 'no'. He said, 'It was most unpleasant, Dad.' So maybe it's better this way...."

"Besides," Elaine piped in, "you've done plenty already. Kevin is there now, isn't he?"

"Yes, he's here. And yes, Karl should have enough for the airporter. He had about $30 when he left and a one way ticket is only about $11. Knowing how he gets food and stuff, he probably hasn't spent much of his money this week." Joni felt a sigh of relief come over the lines. It was the final piece that they needed to trust what Karl had said. They would all know for sure in a matter of hours - once Karl boarded the plane.

"I am just so happy!" Joni was relieved and filled with victory.

"This is just the beginning for us, "said Elaine. "Now it's our turn to be patient with Karl."

"I don't know if we'll be able to care for him," said Donald with a cry in his voice.

"Yes we WILL!" Elaine was adamant.

"I'll be here to give whatever support I can, too," Joni reassured. "You've been there for me all of this time, I intend to do whatever I can to help support the two of you, now, too! No matter how long it takes. We'll all get through this together…and someday we'll all laugh about it, too!"

"Yes, "said Elaine, ever resilient, "and, Joni, we're hoping that you'll be able to come out and visit some time, too. We'd like to see you in person and maybe Karl will want a visit, too."

"I'd like that, too, "said Joni.

She hung up the phone after some tearful goodbyes and lapsed into her 'red letter day feeling'. This chanting stuff really works…she thought to herself and burst into laughter. This was one of her favorite feelings…Victory. It also pointed out to her the futility of doubt, but she knew she would probably have to slay that dragon again and again in the future. For now, this would be a very good day, indeed.

Joni still had most of the clothes she had bought for Karl at her house. In addition, she had much of his writing and books that he enjoyed as well as some art supplies. She would pack a suitcase full of whatever would fit and send it out as soon as possible. She wanted to send some fun things for Karl, as well, so she put in a cheap pair of cool looking sunglasses with a note, 'Karl, your future's so bright, you'll have to wear shades' which was, of course, a line from a song.

As she chanted that evening she realized that some karma had changed and tomorrow would be an auspicious day as well, it was to be Kevin's 16th birthday. She had bought herself some new prayer beads…clear ones and decided that she would switch to them in the morning to celebrate. In addition, she would send her old beads, aqua in color, to Karl with his things because they had been the beads she had used throughout the ordeal. She had never given away a set of her beads before, but it felt right, even if Karl didn't fully appreciate the significance.

Kevin's birthday proved to be another Gale family fun time. They all enjoyed getting together, but it was never a stressful kind of big deal the way most families are. Joni had put up streamers for Kevin's birthday in their apartment, but hadn't had the time or energy to bake a cake. No problem, because Grandma had made a cake and as was her trademark, had tried something new. She had ground chocolate chips and sprinkled them on top of the icing which gave the cake a wonderful textured look. But when Kevin blew out his candles, he blew all of the chocolate off the top of the cake and the whole family roared! Don, Joni's brother-in-law, dubbed it the 'dust bowl cake' and it put everyone in stitches all over again. Well, maybe you had to be there, but it never took much for this family to enjoy a get together. Joni had bought some paper birthday glasses for everyone to wear, instead of hats...and they took lots of silly photos to commemorate the day. She knew it was not the best 16 year old party a kid could want, but then she would take Kevin and Bill and some of his friends to play miniature golf to try to make up for it in a small way. Since Kevin was still legally living in New York, he couldn't go down to the DMV and get his permit, the way most kids would, but nothing seemed to dampen his spirits. At least he never complained to Joni. In terms of family she felt very rich indeed.

She and Kevin rented a movie...later as she did her evening prayers Joni wrote in her journal:

Apr 19

Kevin & I saw "Surviving the Game" - a very violent, action-packed movie, but one I thought was well done. Portrays the evil, dark side of human nature - I now feel it's important to acknowledge and look at that - rather than try to pretend it doesn't exist. In between moments I still feel the empty space that Karl has left - although I try to remember how difficult it was to live with him - haven't cooked dinner all week - I miss that, but since this is Kevin's vacation I'm running him all over town each night.

Then a few days later:

I hope Kevin comes to live. He is really struggling with that decision, I know. I told him at one point that if he ever felt that I was trying to run his life for him - to tell me - because I see that as part of the problem with Karl & his dad - he agreed.

I so want him here, but then I wonder if the strain of leaving his Dad would be too hard. I wonder if he's just trying to please me and make me whole again from losing him. I want him to be whole, but I know he'll be forever divided between us.

Joni had come to feel that intense control over a child could really backlash terribly...was it good instinct or just uneducated guessing? She didn't much care...but she felt strongly that children had to be respected as full human beings.

They chatted in the car all the way to San Francisco. Joni stuffed some cash into Kevin's pocket as they said their goodbyes at the airport. The summer was winding down. After she waited for his plane to take off, Joni walked slowly back to her car. She cried all the way home.

Several days later she was back to her workaday routine.

The call from Kevin was a welcome treat as always. "Hi, Mom! Guess What? I got my permit today!" he was beaming right through the lines. "Dad's taking me out, and Ellie says she'll give me some time, too!"

Joni was happy to hear the news…even though it meant that her baby was growing up. She refused to let any negative thoughts linger, though some danced by her brain. She could have felt sad for all of the time she had missed with him. She could have been resentful that it was his step-mom and not her who would be helping him learn to drive…no wait a minute…that was a benefit! Dirty work she might not even be able to handle! She was genuine in her happiness for him and in her determination to enjoy every moment of time or conversation with him. This part of her would serve her well throughout the rest of her life. The benefit of the nightmare of living apart from him was beginning to show in how she had learned to love him. This was a gift that was far more precious than gold - it was one well earned. She had seen a change that had developed within her life over the years of Buddhist practice. In earlier times, she had wanted to show proof of the practice in a martyred kind of way. She felt that if people understood how badly she had suffered, then her victory would be all the more poignant and sensational. Now she realized she no longer had the desire to cull sympathy. She was capable of truly enjoying what there was to enjoy in her life. This didn't mean an avoidance or dismissal of the negatives; just an acknowledgment that though they existed, they were no longer the center of her life. She was truly free.

"Hi Joni!" It was Elaine on the phone, with Donald on the extension. "We thought we'd give a call now because Karl has gone out for a walk…we were able to get him signed up for Medicaid, finally. It was pretty awful because at one point he realized that we were saying he was mentally ill and became very agitated. He said, 'I'm not crazy! There's nothing wrong with me! I can work!' and then went for a walk. He came back, though. Honestly, Joni, we wouldn't have been able to deal with him if it wasn't for your help!"

"Oh, I'm so glad you were able to accomplish that! I'm more than happy to have been even a small part in all of this! Thank you!" Joni was truly happy that they had at least the financial basis for Karl's care in place. If he were to then run away or anything, it would be that much easier for him to receive help if he was already in the system. She was still skeptical as to whether Karl would go in voluntarily. It seemed as though a major trauma of some kind would have to ensue in order for him to be forced into care.

The reality that the three of them knew was that he was not able to work ...but if he were to try, it might bring the point to the surface of his consciousness, too.

They talked a bit longer, the parents promising to keep Joni posted. Joni continuing to pledge whatever support she could lend. They asked for copies of Karl's writings and paintings to be sent to a psychiatrist there. Joni complied.

Joni was now out of it and the next miracle would have to begin in Minnesota. All that she could do was pray for their success and happiness. She was drifting out of the mainstream of the case and it felt completely right. As time and distance passed, she wondered what would have happened if the whole thing had gone on any longer for her. Would she, too be facing anti-psychotic medication? In fact, some of her friends had held their breath for her and she knew it. But, like a child climbing atop a high jungle gym to the terrified audience of parents below, she had felt safe at every step. What's more, she had made it through with barely a scratch.

Elaine and Donald called on occasion. Joni looked forward to any news they had, but Karl refused to talk to her. She didn't mind. The picture of what was going on there wasn't rosy at all; Karl shoplifting and Donald bringing him back to the store and paying for the items (shaving stuff, mainly), Elaine and Donald asking Karl to let his hair grow - Karl shaving his head, Elaine and Donald asking Karl to get help - Karl bolting out of the house for hours in the cold - Donald driving around trying to find him. The window of Karl's awareness that he needed help now iced over by many realities: he was back home with his parents, he was no longer a child, he was incapable of living the life of a normal 31 year old man, but most importantly, the whole Samadhi thing was probably a hoax...and had been all these years.

Elaine and Donald would call with his latest attitude problem or behavior and ask Joni if it had been manifest when he lived with her. She would offer what she could as to what she knew...and they would compare notes. One thing was obvious; the road to professional help for Karl was not going to be a 'freeway'. Karl was still refusing help.

In an effort to appease and perhaps acclimate him to the area, Donald brought him with him to the University and Karl would spend time in the library and on the quad.

Soon, though, he was caught shoplifting some pens from the bookstore. Donald was humiliated and had to stop letting Karl be on campus unattended. Elaine was keeping up with her full time job and doing her best to work around Karl's attitudes and moods. She was particularly disturbed by his sleeplessness and poor appetite. She was also marvelously delighted whenever Karl's old wit and humor surfaced. These were rare occasions, but one crumb of hope could feed a village of fears by this time.

They had ministers and psychologists visit, but the work of getting Karl to accept help was more than a full time job in itself. Joni did not envy them their dilemma. They were even more grateful for what she had endured before them. Admiration and support all around.

Time passed a bit more quickly for Joni, now. She knew that it had slowed down a bit for Elaine and Donald, but she also felt that time was on their side. She sent cards to Karl and to Elaine and Donald, as well. Karl never answered, but, Joni wasn't really expecting he would. The harshness of what had really been his life would be hard to face with the return of sanity…and he wasn't even close to that yet.

Her note inside the card of 5/6/94 read:

Dearest Karl,

How are you? I hope all is well and that you are gaining a new lease on life!

Did you see the eclipse today? It was only a partial out here - plus there's too much fog.

Do you remember old Bob from Steamers? They've written a book about the WWII plane he flew and it's dedicated to him! He may be coming to Minneapolis for a book signing - I told him to take me along - that I'd go and see you! (Don't think <u>that</u> will happen!) Anyway, a doctor in Minneapolis now owns the plane and flies it in shows! If I ever get my hands on a copy of the book I'll send you one - so far I can't locate it!

Your folks tell me you shoveled snow a few weeks ago! It's hard to believe there is still snow falling at this time of year, but it is! I used to enjoy shoveling snow. (weird, huh?)

Well, honey, I hope you'll write to me some time. You're also welcome to call collect any time.

Kevin is due out for the summer in early July. Not sure if he'll come to live - he goes back and forth on that one. We'll see.

<u>Take care!</u>

264

Love, Joni

Elaine and Donald had begun to go to counseling even though Karl would not attend.

Joni was very supportive and had encouraged the idea. As she wrote to Elaine the following week, she tried to be honest with her feelings without sounding preachy. As she read over her lines, she seemed to have fallen short on both counts, but she took the chance and mailed the letter, anyway.

5/13/94

Dear Elaine,

Sorry our conversation was interrupted so many times - I just wanted to let you know that my prayers are with you.

Karl is trying hard to retain his independence as a man - but because he's in the powerless situation of not being able to fully care for himself, his only way to assert himself is through disappearing on you for a time or not complying with household rules.

In his heart, he's confused by his own feelings - and very afraid. Somehow, I hope, he will be able to break through and express his rage and frustration in a controlled setting. I know he's "in there" even though he withdraws.

Trust with all your heart and life that he will progress - and try to see him as a man in conflict with himself rather than as your son. He needs to feel autonomous, but is smart enough to know he's dependent and that discourages him.

Of course, you and Donald need to set whatever household rules you need to stay sane - but if he can't follow them or refuses to; you may have to consider alternatives to having him live with you.

I'm sure that this will have a happy ending. You & Donald are doing a great thing by going to counseling yourselves even without his participation, yet. This will help him immeasurably even though it may not be apparent as yet.

Will keep in touch. I love you all! Love and light,

Joni

"Sanity is a cozy lie."

-Susan Sontag

Chapter Fifteen   Full Circle

Joni began to write at the desk she had set up for Karl. She hung his "Hair-brained" picture on the wall. It's orange and yellow fire a screaming reminder of the path that she had walked. A new awareness of her life was unfolding. She sat in the spot that faced the window onto a beautiful, tree-filled front lawn. She saw through the window with new colors in her eyes. She sat at the desk and the place seemed right to write - which was what she knew she had to do. And now, there was time to do it. She sat in the spot, in the place, at the desk and she began again. That had now become her theme stance...beginning again, but it was okay now. She wasn't fighting it this time. She wasn't wasting the time it took to get from denial to fighting to acceptance - she just accepted. It was time.

Her thoughts conflicted as she wrote. Could she tell it all? Should she protect the innocent? And what of the not-so-innocent? Did they deserve protection, too? Was it all too risky, or boring? Who cared? The time, the space, the will, the place, had come together for a breathless moment and she was ready.

Her letters to Karl were short and fairly frequent, but they were never answered. So she was writing to herself in a way. She worked through her feelings - knowing how illogical they were - yet somehow still captive to them. Distractions and confusion seemed to help. So she dated and placed personal ads. Went on dates with nice men like Joe who took her to dinner and dancing. Wonderful and fun times, but her heart wasn't free. Stupid she thought. Stupid she *knew.* But, this was all there was right now.

After two dates with Joe she cut it off; afraid that the big 'S' question would come up.

She didn't want that much involvement and didn't want to explain herself. Her mind would detach every now and then, though and she would remember something that she needed to tell Minnesota. Karl is a time-bomb waiting to go off, she would say.

"Can't you talk about something else?" Chris was annoyed with her, but trying to keep his anger in as he knew the tightrope he was walking.

"You know I can't help it." Joni said with real apology in her voice. "It's just something that I needed to do…and now I just want to help in any way that I can until this thing comes to a happy conclusion." They both knew that underneath her gentle apology was a she-cat ready to pounce if pressed to abandon her course in any way.

"You know you look beautiful tonight," Chris tactfully changed the subject, "Let's dance."

Joni smiled and put her hand into his as they walked to the floor. This was a new experience for her. She had never really been to this place, even though it was closest to her house. They were in a tiny local bar with a dance floor big

268

enough for four couples, max. There was a live band, but only one couple was free style dancing. So as she and Chris started dancing, they were the obvious couple to watch. It seemed to entertain the lonely band members and they enjoyed their chance to show off, but left early to go home and be together.

Maybe it was a lingering sensation from the oppression of the dark and thick-aired bar, or maybe just a culmination of things, but Joni ended up in tears. Chris's forte was patience and his talent for communication came like a skilled craftsman. Joni soon spilled her guts. With his help she understood her problem.

"Chris, thank you for your patience. You're so good at communication, you don't know..."

"Joni, just tell me what it is you're feeling. Go ahead, I can take it." Chris was firm, but obviously anxious to know the source of her distress.

Joni started, trying again and again to look at him as she spoke, but her head kept bowing with the weight of her tears. "It's just that...I know that I'm your first, but I won't be your last....and that's what I realize I am really looking for...to be someone's *last*."

"How do you know you wouldn't be my last? What if I were to marry you?" Chris was defending himself and it carried a weak tone that grated on Joni and confirmed her own thoughts.

"C'mon, Chris. You know that that isn't going to happen. You're going to want children and all of that; I've already raised mine."

"How do you know? How do you know?" Chris had become indignant. "I think I might want kids, but it sure doesn't seem like that's going to happen for me now. I'm already 27 and women my age just don't appeal to me. I can't help it...I've tried, but I just feel more comfortable with older women. So, whether you like it or not...the fact is that I probably *won't* have kids...and it won't be your fault if I don't. I'm making a conscious decision based on where I feel comfortable. Is that so hard to understand?"

"No. But..."

"Don't give me any 'buts'! I'm capable of deciding this for myself! I love you and I want to be with you and you need to quit trying to take responsibility for my life. Isn't that what you always say anyway? People have to be responsible for their own lives?" His voice was now a shout and Joni was feeling that uncomfortable blush come to her cheeks.

"Ssssh! Chris, I get your point. And you're right, but let's keep our voices level, okay? I don't want my neighbors to hear this whole thing."

"Okay, sorry."

"But, you're right. Absolutely, you have the right to decide about your own life and there's nothing wrong with wanting to be with older women, but that is subject to change, too. There are lots of reasons why it won't work for us - but the main one is that although I feel love for you, as I've told you from the beginning, I am not in love with you. If I could be, I would. In fact, if I could it would solve all of my problems...you're a good man and you communicate so well, that any woman would be lucky to have you. But, I'm not and I can't seem to change that. But most of all, our lives are going in different directions, I wish you could see that."

"You know, Joni, I don't get it! You just close yourself off behind this big wall. I hate when you do that!" Chris was irate.

"Why can't we try? Why can't we just relax and try this? You know there are a lot of reasons that we are good together, too. You've said it yourself…"

Joni cut him off, "Look, Chris, I can't keep going around and around on this. I just can't do it."

The argument died an unsettled death and the day went mercifully on. Joni's mind never stopped working on the problem at hand; how to get out of this mess she'd gotten herself into.

It was comical on the surface. *No wonder I'm more comfortable with crazy people,* she thought to herself. *I can't seem to get through to normal folks…can't seem to have a normal relationship & life…always have to complicate things. Oi vey!* Was there some kind of law at work here? One that said…if you're attracted to someone, they won't be attracted to you and vice versa? It seemed to be that way…always.
But more was afoot and the problem of not being able to fall in love properly would soon be dwarfed by other changes.

Kevin called and said he did want to live with her in California and that he was not going to go back to New York after summer vacation. Joni's boss, Jack told her that he was taking a job with a local hospital and would be closing his office. Wayne had quit work at Steamers after a dispute in which he had been cut out of a potential deal to buy the place. Within the space of one week, Joni felt the earth shift on its axis. The time spent dancing with 'Jesus' had ended just in time. Now the world would be different.

Joni enjoyed the next few weeks with Chris. They had lots of good times, even though she was determined not to make him a 'steady'. She dated a few other men, but none seriously; she was gearing up for her son to be with her again and holding her breath that it might be a permanent change!

271

She wanted to put the majority of her energy into being a mother again.

Chris didn't want to let her go. Kevin's father didn't want to let him go. There was wailing and crying and gnashing of teeth, but she did, and so did he. Mother and son were again united; it was right.

Joni found herself going into business for herself. Still working for the doctor, but knowing that the hours would be diminishing rapidly, she began her search for new possibilities. Many job applications went unanswered. Few interviews came, and Joni's dad had swung into action trying to price office space for rent, etc.

In the midst of this Joni's letters to Karl became sparser as did the responses from Elaine and Donald. Elaine's dad died in mid-June.

By early July Wayne had bought a new club and named it Kodiak Jack's. It was like a phoenix rising from the ashes.

By mid-July Karl had agreed to get help and was admitted to a psychiatric ward.

Elaine and Donald's letter chronicled the events this way:

Dearest Friends,

Karl has refused to cooperate or go for help because "there's nothing wrong with him." He has been home three months. The Lord has been leading us every step of the way as He performs a miracle. This is a short chronology of "part of Karl's journey." We want to share with you God's goodness—answers to all of our prayers!

The Fourth of July weekend at the cabin was a real disaster. Karl insisted on swimming out into all the boat traffic on the lake. He had no idea how dangerous it was. When he was being lectured to on the dock, he turned to walk away running right into David. He pushed David giving him a threatening look of pure hate. That's why we lock our doors!

During the week following the swimming episode, Donald contacted Dr. Erdman for a second opinion about asking Karl to leave our house. (We had been advised by the Pyramid therapists to put Karl back on the streets because we were enabling him.)

Dr. Erdman suggested setting Karl up in an apartment for a month if he would not go for help.

Elaine contacted a Christian psychiatrist to discuss deliverance. He assured her that before Karl can even want to be right with the Lord, he needs medication to think clearly. God does not force Himself on anyone. He has to be a choice. Clearly we cannot help Karl here at home.

We called pre-petition screening for the third time and were turned down for the third time. Karl is "not a danger to himself or others."

Thursday night (7-7) we gave Karl his options: get a job, go for help or leave. He signed a statement that he would not work, so we decided not to set him up in an apartment. He agreed to leave at 10:00 on Friday morning. We asked him to go right away. He said he would be glad to be rid of us and left. (This was unbelievably hard to go through.)

Elaine drove after him to give him his HCMA card. Karl was already coming back because it had started to rain. We said that he could come home for the night.

Things went on as usual until mid-morning the next day. At 10:00 Saturday Elaine asked him to take a warm coat and some food. He said, "You're really serious about this, aren't you?" he left then stating that he would never see us again. God had other plans: at 12:00 noon Karl walked in the back door saying, "Take me to a psychiatrist." Donald called Dr. Erdman who set us up with the HCMC Crisis Center. We drove Karl down at 2:00. He was seen by an admitting nurse. Karl readily spilled his guts about what was going on in his head. He was all set to "prove" that there was nothing wrong with him. We left there at 3:00. He was admitted for a 72 hour hold.

On Monday (7-11) we were notified that Karl's release time was to be Wednesday (7-13) at 4:50 PM. It was a probability that they would not keep Karl because he was refusing help and medication.

We called Karl on Monday night to express our concern that he was not cooperating and we don't want to see him on the streets again. He hung up on us. Karl felt that we had treated him cruelly and without respect.

Elaine manned the phone Tuesday (7-12) morning. Dr. Kim called saying that he would press for an evaluation. The pre-petition screener, Dr. Long, interviewed her at length saying that Karl still was not a danger to himself or others. He met the other two conditions for involuntary commitment: medical diagnosis and inability to care for himself.

God worked miraculously on Wednesday (7-14) changing a negative pre-petition report into a recommendation for commitment.

Both psychiatrists, Dr. Pearson and Dr. Kim, supported Karl's need to receive an evaluation and treatment immediately. Judge Debbie Hedland called Jim Alcrect at the County Attorney's office supporting it. (We did, too.) In the meantime,

Dr. Long called Joni Mathews in California to confirm Karl's minor assault on her (4-11) which changed his mind. This was sufficient evidence of "clear and present danger."

Right now Karl is being held at HCMC and will be getting the psychiatric help he do desperately needs. This is another beginning for Karl. God is bringing him closer and closer to Himself. It's truly a miracle! We are anxious to share this latest development/answer to our prayers and to thank each of you for praying. Karl will be a testimony of God's everlasting love!

We praise the Lord with thankful hearts. Your friends in Christ, Elaine and Donald

Joni felt thrilled that she had participated in getting Karl to help. She felt trepidation at the treatment she knew would have to follow. Would he be cured? Would he emerge as she had envisioned, a man capable of creating meaning and value in his life? Would all that would befall him in the name of mercy be more horrific than the disease itself?

But then, her part was done. Whether she had in actuality created a haven or a deeper hell, she could only know that her *intention* was clear and right, based on respect and love.

She spent the next month in a whirlwind of change. Had to go to court (via New York State) for a judge to rule that Kevin could live with her as his dad was blocking the switch. Kevin won and was granted the right to stay in California with her. Victory! She closed down the office where she had worked for the doctor for the previous 7 years and moved into a makeshift office in the tack room of his horse barn. It was a major shock to her system, but no other job offers were panning out; plus, she was still needed by the doctor for coordinating parts of his schedule and work. Meanwhile she was able to pick up more bookkeeping clients to fill out her work week. She now had a telephone installer and a vineyard owner as clients. She met a new man and began a new love relationship.

In the midst of her life and changes with regard to new full-time mother status, new downsized job and new love relationship, Joni became ill. She was now dragging herself to work each day and leaving about halfway through. She slept a lot and tried to keep positive thoughts of health. In the meantime, she lost track of Karl's status until a call came from Donald and Elaine. Karl had been out on one of his weekend visits with them and apparently had asked to live with them. They had felt that he needed more time with treatment as his doctors had ordered. This upset Karl and when he was back in the institution he slit both of his wrists. Donald said that he had called out for help and that's what saved him and that they had put both of his arms in casts as a precautionary measure.

"I think we should be able to sue them for this," Donald was saying, "They knew he was suicidal, he should have been watched."

Joni's eyes felt hot and her jaw clenched. Sorrow mixed with anger and disgust. She had come to care for Elaine and Donald, but Donald's litigious nature grated on her nerves. She said nothing about it directly, but offered, "I'm glad he's going to be okay. That's the main thing. Thanks so much for letting me know, too, I really appreciate it."

She later wrote in her journal about how she felt that the idea of blaming others for problems in this way was a major portion of Karl's distorted view of the world. Taken to extremes, blaming others for every mishap or misadventure is schizophrenic in itself, she thought. Despite this she wrote to them:

10/19/94

276

Dear Donald & Elaine,

Thank you so much for letting me know about Karl's condition. I have written him a short note also. Frankly, I feel out of touch - out of ideas. I don't quite know what to do for him anymore - other than to pray for him and for your entire family.

I've offered to keep up a correspondence with him - should he want that, but so far I haven't had much feedback from him at all. My life continues to move on - but I will never write him off. Let me know if there is <u>anything</u> at all that I can do to help in this situation. Thank you for your continued friendship.

Love, Joni

Deciding to face the truth head-on with Karl she wrote to him, also:

Dear Karl,

I was saddened to hear of your suicide attempt. I hope that you will be able to talk with people that are near to you there. Also, I would be more than happy to keep up a correspondence with you - should you want to write.

Karl, I know you're struggling to come to terms with Truth and Life. Please know that I care for you and that I am always willing to listen. You must choose to live long enough to understand your life and turn all of your struggles into a crowning victory! You have tremendous courage!

Love, Joni

Kevin had been acting out in school, disrupting class with Beavis & Butthead cartoon imitations. Joni was now in full swing as a mother of a teen, and she had so little energy. Her weakness lasted an unprecedented six weeks. It was a joyous feeling at the end of it to feel alive again.

Before she knew it, December had rolled in and she got a Christmas card and letter from Karl's parents.

15 Dec 1994

Dear Joni:

Sorry we haven't contacted you for a while. We get awfully busy even without the problem with Karl. I am just finishing up the two books I have been working on. Hard to keep it all going as we have rather heavy teaching loads at the community college also. Karl has been with us again for nearly one month. The roller coaster effect still exists. He is making gains gradually but his stubbornness and self-centeredness continue. Once in a while there is a sign of change though and that is encouraging. The problem we had this past two weeks was that we suspected he had decided not to take his antipsychotic drug and antidepressant. Elaine began to count pills and we were correct. He began to seem too depressed and worried us when we had to leave him home alone. On a Monday night when I was teaching, Elaine also had a Bible study group. He had to be alone. I called home twice in the evening to check on him. He did not answer the phone. When finally I went home, I was afraid to go in the house for fear he had taken his life. Well, he was lying on the couch watching TV and all kinds of messages had piled up on the answering machine. I asked why he hadn't answered the phone. His reply was, "I didn't think anyone wanted to talk to me." Karl does not believe in God now because, "if there was a God, He wouldn't have allowed me to maim my wrists as I did" So, within one year, he has gone from believing he was God to where there can't be one. Amazing isn't it? He continues to be obsessed with what he did to his wrists and how he has destroyed part of himself.

278

I called his social worker to tell her we had discovered he had not been taking his meds. They also discovered he was anemic and is taking iron. She said to tell him that from now on, as a condition of his commitment, he must take the meds in front of us. He is doing that. I explained to her that we couldn't cope with the depression and the fears of what he might do in that state. We also explained that to Karl and that he would have to be taken back to the crisis center if he did not cooperate.

Karl continues making plans to go back to school (graduate school) in the fall. We hope, of course, that he will be ready to do that. We wouldn't mind if he stayed here while he does that but he will not be allowed to if he doesn't begin to assume a more helpful role. It isn't much to ask for what he gets while here. He may catch on eventually. Neither Elaine nor I have a desire to continue waiting on him hand and foot at his age. To have to tell him every time he can't see when something needs doing (making the bed, doing his wash, helping with cleaning and dishes) gets old.

Furthermore, it isn't good for him. He likes to lie on the couch and watch TV, particularly 9-11 each evening when a local channel plays two one-hour Star Trek shows. He is a "Trekkie" now.

Karl's weekly schedule is as follows right now: MWF he buses to Eden Prairie to work for Phil Vann. He has done that about five days now. Phil is the man who was captured by the Viet Cong for two and one-half years, disemboweled and had electrodes hooked to his testes. I may have told you about him. Surviving all that, he got into the drug scene, attempted suicide about four times, robbed 29 banks, had four marriages and finally served a prison term where he met his present wife. She was in for embezzling from a bank. It was a Bible and two other vets (from our church Vet's Club, one the arresting officer) in a jail cell that turned Phil's life around. He and Cindy have it all together now. He came immediately the night of Karl's attempt. He showed Karl the scars on his wrists and described his failed attempts at carbon monoxide poisoning. Most of all, he showed a lot of love for Karl. Phil told him that night he had a job when he needed it. Phil has known about this situation for about three years. Karl had asked for Phil to come but doesn't remember asking.

He and Cindy have a million dollar business going now. Karl's social worker feels he is the ideal person to be talking to Karl. Phil has taken him aside and talked to him about taking medication and his wrists since we have had this problem. On the bright side, Phil called a couple days ago to tell me that Karl is an outstanding worker and even more that he yuks it up with the guys through the day and really seems to enjoy being there. They are having an office party this Friday evening and Karl really wants to go. Another fellow in the office picks Karl up and returns him as he lives near here. He is also in our church Vet's Club with Phil and I. Isn't it odd how, looking back, people have entered Karl's life to move the situation slowly toward the positive with us there constantly trying. Thank God for you and the role you played. It was so easy to visualize losing our son out there on the street. You turned out to be the angel in Karl's life. Perhaps one day he will recognize that. The role Phil is playing is also occurring with the right timing. Anyway, on TR, Karl busses to Minneapolis and engages in the therapy groups as usual. He is working on a set of chessmen in one session. He is at the painting stage now. I have gotten a couple computer chess games for him. The computer gets a lot of rest now as Karl no longer writes the scriptures for God. He has a lot of angry feelings towards Easwaran.

Another really strange thing about the day Karl attempted suicide: Karl asked for Phil to come in late afternoon. Our pastor had been with us all afternoon. When I called Phil, they were out to eat and so I left a message for him which he did get but they had to stop and eat on the way to the hospital. Our pastor, stopping to eat on the way home from being with us, by chance met Phil and Cindy in the restaurant. He did share with Phil as pastor and is also one of us in Vet's Club. Phil knew about Karl, but pastor did not know that he did. Phil, Cindy and the three kids were on their way to the hospital anyway. But, this took place in a large city after chance meeting in the same restaurant.

If this eventually has a happy ending you know you played a BIG part in it.

All the children will be here for X-mas. Karl isn't really into the giving as we would like him to be but he is in the drawing the children have between them. Jill and husband Bob, Jeff and Angie with their brood (Cory, Bradley & Elizabeth), and David will be home. Think where it all was one year ago. I remember being so thankful he was under your wing at X-mas and not on the street. Have you ever been able to share with Bucko and the others as to where this has gone? I think now there is a good chance that one day, Karl will give us reason to be very proud. We have a long way to go but now seem to have a good start.

You must be tired of reading so I will sign off for now. Drop a line. We haven't forgotten you by any means. Hope you and Kevin have a grand X-mas. Wish it weren't so far, we would drop in for a visit. Perhaps someday we can do that. We like to travel.

Take care and God Bless you,

Elaine and Donald

Joni was now settled in to her life as an independent contractor and had plenty of work. Wayne hired her to help set up the books for the club and he's have her do the payroll and year end reports. Kevin was home for good and in school. He

281

brought his buddies by for dinner some nights, others he'd be out cruisin' with them. She had broken up with her last boyfriend – he had been toxic for her. She felt sick almost the entire time he was in her life. It was time to start dancing again.

She sat at a table in Kodiak Jack's waiting for the dancing to begin. Her diet coke and a pitcher of water in the middle – which she'd share with the other regulars who would sit with her. While she waited, she pulled a letter out of her purse that she had gotten that day from Elaine & Donald. It was already October, two years had passed since she took Karl in. His parents' letters were fewer and farther between.

Karl had applied to three universities and had been accepted by all three with offers of scholarships ranging from $10,000 to $14,000. He was majoring in microbial genetics, his post-graduate work. He was off all of his medications. The doctors had never seen such tremendous progress in a case such as his. Socially he remained a bit awkward according to Donald and Elaine, but he was receiving 'A's in his classes and also earning money through his work.

The music started – Joni jumped up with a smile and took her place on the dance floor. The letter half-stuffed into her purse, slipped down
         to the dark place
                  on the floor
                           under the table.